The Trainer's Handbook

Karen Lawson

Jossey-Bass
Pfeiffer

San Francisco

7-23-99

Copyright © 1998 by Karen Lawson

ISBN:0-7879-3991-9

Lawson, Karen
    The trainer's handbook
    Karen Lawson.—1st. ed.
    p. cm.
    Includes bibliographical references and index.
    ISBN 0-7879-3991-9
      1. Employees—training of—Handbooks, manuals, etc.
      2. Training—Handbooks, manuals, etc. I. Title.
HF5549.5.T7L344   1998   98-5369
658.3'1243—dc21

Printed in the United States of America
Published by

350 Sansome Street, 5th Floor
San Francisco, California 94104-1342
(415) 433-1740; Fax (415) 433-0499
(800) 274-4434; Fax (800) 569-0443

Visit our website at: www.pfeiffer.com

Outside of the United States, Pfeiffer products can be purchased from the following Simon & Schuster International Offices:

Simon & Schuster (Asia) Pte Ltd
317 Alexandra Road
#04-01 IKEA Building
Singapore 15996
Asia
65 476 4688; Fax 65 378 0370

Prentice Hall Professional
Locked Bag 506
Frenchs Forest PO NSW 2086
Australia
61 29454 2200; Fax 61 29453 0089

Prentice Hall
Campus 400
Maylands Avenue
Hempel Hempstead5
Hertfordshire HP2 7EZ
United Kingdom
44(0) 1442 881891; Fax 44(0) 1442 882074

Prentice Hall/Pfeiffer
P.O. Box 1636
Randburg 2125
South Africa
27 11 781 0780; Fax 27 11 781 0781

Jossey-Bass/Pfeiffer
3255 Wyandotte Street east
Windsor, Ontario N8Y 1E9
Canada
888-866-5559: Fax 61 2 9453 0089

Acquiring Editor: Matt Holt
Director of Development: Kathleen Dolan Davies
Developmental Editor: Carol Nolde
Editor: Rebecca Taff
Senior Production Editor: Dawn Kilgore
Interior Design: Joseph Piliero
Cover Design: Laura Glazer
Production: Publication Services

Printing 10 9 8 7 6 5 4 3 2 1

*To Mel Silberman, my mentor,
teacher, colleague, and friend.*

Contents

Figures and Exhibits

Preface

The field of training and development is growing by leaps and bounds. Along with the growth of the industry has come the demand for more and better-trained trainers. For the purposes of this book, "trainer" refers very broadly to *anyone who is responsible for delivering instruction to adult learners*. A trainer might be (1) an internal HRD professional employed by an organization and responsible for providing training to the organization's employees; (2) a subject-matter expert who has been enlisted as a full-time professional trainer; (3) one who delivers training on a part-time basis as part of his or her overall job responsibilities; or (4) a practitioner who contracts with an organization to design and/or deliver training programs. Often an external trainer is a casualty of another corporation's downsizing or perhaps someone who just wanted a career change. In either case, this individual has turned to the training profession as a means of utilizing skills or expertise in a particular discipline or subject area.

Internal or external, full-time or part-time, the demand for trainers often exceeds the supply, so to meet their needs, organizations often turn to those in line positions. These subject-matter experts are expected to deliver training, not just present information. Unfortunately, these folks have received little or no formal instruction on how to train. They are thrown into the position and left to sink or swim. They find themselves training the way they themselves were trained. In many situations, that means a didactic approach in which the trainer stands in front of participants and dumps information on often-unhearing ears.

Although the didactic approach never did work as the sole method for training adult learners, it is even less effective today because trainers are no longer viewed as merely disseminators of information. They are expected to be facilitators, agents of learning, and performance consultants. These roles require them to move away from specific task-oriented instruction and to concentrate on helping people and organizations improve performance.

Trainers need to design, develop, and deliver training that encourages people at all levels of the organization to take responsibility for their own learning. The trainer is required to be a catalyst, a resource person, and often a coach, to help people through the discovery process.

The effective trainer also has to understand business needs and identify for participants how those needs are linked to learning and performance needs. Quite simply, the purpose of most corporate training is to help line managers solve business problems. Trainers must learn how to develop partnerships with managers, who are ultimately accountable for the success of training. Before this can happen, however, trainers must become proficient at the skills and competencies that define them as professional trainers. As with any profession, they are required to master a certain body of knowledge and set of skills. To that end, this book provides both novice and experienced trainers with a comprehensive set of tools to develop training skills and competencies.

Those who are thrown into full-time, professional training positions with little or no formal training can use this book to learn the fundamentals of training or supplement what they already know. They can come up to speed in a relatively short period of time. Experienced trainers will gain new tips and techniques to enhance their current skills and help them deliver on-target training that meets individual as well as organizational needs.

The book includes checklists, forms, and specific activities that trainers can use immediately in designing, developing, and delivering their own training programs.

This handbook can stand alone or be used in conjunction with the Instructor's Guide, which provides a complete step-by-step process for conducting an effective, interactive train-the-trainer program.

April 1998

Karen Lawson
Lansdale, Pennsylvania

Acknowledgments

I would like to thank the many people who have attended my training sessions throughout the years. In essence, they are the authors of this book. They have taught me what it means to be a training professional.

I also wish to acknowledge Dr. Roger Raber and Mary Johnston for giving me my first train-the-trainer opportunity and to Gloria Becker for her encouragement and support during my trial-and-error period.

I am grateful to the many training professionals who have shared their tips and techniques from conference platforms and also one-on-one. Many of these colleagues have become my close friends. In particular, I thank Steve Sugar for his willingness to share ideas and materials. I also thank my dear friend, Harriet Rifkin, with whom I have shared the joy and pain of growing as a training professional, for her caring and sharing.

I particularly thank Dr. Mel Silberman for the many growth opportunities we have shared over the past six years. His influence has truly made a difference in my life.

My heartfelt appreciation goes to Carol Hunsberger for her hours of proofreading and editorial assistance. I also wish to thank my mother, Mildred Eells, for her weekly words of encouragement.

Finally, to my husband, Bob Lawson: I can never adequately express how much I appreciate his love and support throughout the years. I thank him not only for his patience and understanding but for his belief in me even when I didn't believe in myself. He is my colleague and partner, my champion and much-needed critic, but most of all, he is my best friend.

About the Author

Karen Lawson is an international consultant, speaker, and writer. As founder and president of Lawson Consulting Group, she has built a successful consulting firm specializing in organization and management development. She has extensive consulting and workshop experience in the areas of management, team development, communication, and quality service across a wide range of industries, including financial services, pharmaceutical, health care, government, and nonprofit organizations.

In her consulting work with Fortune 500 companies as well as small businesses, she uses her experience and knowledge of human relations to help leaders at all levels make a difference in their organizations. She has held many key leadership positions in professional organizations, including the American Society for Training and Development (ASTD) and the National Speakers Association (NSA). She has also received numerous professional awards for her contributions to the training profession.

Lawson holds a doctorate in adult and organizational development from Temple University. She earned her M.A. from the University of Akron and B.A. from Mount Union College. She is also a graduate of the National School of Banking in Fairfield, Connecticut.

She is the author of *The Art of Influencing, Improving Workplace Performance Through Coaching, Improving On-the-Job Training and Coaching*, and *Involving Your Audience – Make It Active*. She is the co-author of *101 Ways To Make Training Active* and has published dozens of articles in professional journals. She has presented at many regional and national professional conferences and is on the adjunct faculty of several colleges and universities, including the University of Delaware and Villanova University.

Introduction

The success of any training program or initiative depends on your using a systematic approach to delivering effective instruction with high impact for both the participants and the organization. To that end, you, as the trainer, must understand various principles and concepts of learning and also follow a process that results in behavioral change. This process (reflected by the arrangement of this book) consists of five parts: *analysis*, *design*, *development*, *delivery*, and *evaluation*.

The analysis phase is covered in Modules One through Four. In Module One, you will learn how to conduct a needs analysis at both the organizational and individual levels. Module Two addresses the principles of adult learning as well as learning styles. You will have an opportunity to learn about your own personal training style in Module Three. To round out the analysis phase, Module Four provides additional insights and understanding of the complexity and diversity of today's training environment.

The second phase in the design process is addressed in the next two modules. Module Five explains how to write training objectives, and Module Six presents a step-by-step approach to developing a complete instructional plan.

After the program has been designed, the next step is to fully develop the program, selecting and creating activities and tools to create an exciting and effective learning experience. You will learn about specific active-training methods and techniques in Module Seven.

The next step in the instructional process is delivery. Modules Eight through Eleven give creative tips and techniques for delivering a dynamic and professional training session. You will also learn how to deal with difficult people and situations.

Finally, in Module Twelve you will learn how to evaluate training and measure its effectiveness. You will learn how to go beyond the "smile sheet" at the end of a session and develop more tools and techniques to show the benefits of training to employees and the organization.

By developing your skills in each of these five areas, you will indeed become a master of your craft.

Module One

Assessing Needs

LEARNING OUTCOMES

In this module, you will learn

- To identify key steps in the needs-assessment process
- To select appropriate methods to gather data
- To develop questions for a variety of needs-assessment techniques
- To apply the needs-assessment process to a specific organization and situation

---

UNDERSTANDING NEEDS ASSESSMENT

Every year companies spend thousands and thousands of dollars on training programs that fail. Why? Because they do not meet the specific business needs of the organization and the specific professional development needs of employees.

A needs assessment is the core of any training program. It gives the basis for program development and establishes the criteria for measuring the success of the program after its completion.

Defining Needs Assessment

Needs assessors are much like physicians who ask a series of questions and order a battery of medical tests to uncover and treat the causes rather than the symptoms of an ailment. Needs assessment is the process of determining the cause, extent, and appropriate cure for organizational ills. The process addresses the organizational context and combines organizational analysis, data gathering, and interviewing techniques to identify and shrink the gap between desired and actual knowledge, skills, and performance. It is

1

a careful study of the organizational context, the job itself, and the knowledge, skills, and abilities of the job incumbents.

Simply put, the process identifies both the desired performance and the current performance. The difference, the gap between the actual and the desired level of performance, becomes the training need and provides the basis for the training design. Correct problem identification (cause) is the key to developing and implementing appropriate corrective measures (cure).

Using Needs Assessment

Before we address *how* to conduct a needs assessment, we must look at the reasons for doing one. Overall, the purpose of a needs assessment is to prevent a quick-fix, bandage approach to business problems. Instead, a needs assessment, if done properly, will ensure that the solution(s) addresses the real issue(s) and effectively focuses the appropriate resources, time, and effort toward a targeted solution. The following are some valid reasons for conducting a needs assessment.

To Determine Whether Training Is Needed Poor performance is not always a training issue. Often performance problems are the result of poor management practices, organizational barriers, or inadequate systems or equipment. A needs assessment, if conducted properly, will determine whether training is necessary and avoid the mistake of applying a training solution to a non-training problem. If it is determined that the problem does require training, the needs assessment will help identify the performance issues that training should address.

To Determine Causes of Poor Performance As noted above, poor performance can be the result of many other factors, including poor incentives, lack of internal motivation, the work environment, inadequate skills and knowledge, or the employees' lack of confidence. Sometimes, the cause may be poor management practices, such as poor hiring decisions, poor communication, unclear expectations, or inadequate coaching and feedback. There is a saying that "Ducks don't climb trees." Unfortunately, corporations are full of "ducks" in positions that require "cats," and no matter how hard they try, they will never succeed in their positions. If employees are put in positions for which they are unsuited, all the training in the world will not improve their performance. In other cases, managers fail their employees by not stating clearly their expectations or standards of performance.

Often, employees do not know what is expected of them. They may have the knowledge, skills, and ability to do the job quite well but are not meeting the manager's expectations. If that is the case, then the training should be directed toward the manager rather than the manager's employees.

To *Determine Content and Scope of Training* A needs assessment will help determine the type of training necessary to achieve results. Should it be workshop, self-study, or on-the-job? It will help to identify how long the training program should be and who the target audience should be. It will also help identify what should be included in the program and the degree of urgency.

To *Determine Desired Training Outcomes* The needs assessment will help to determine what knowledge, skills, and attitudes must be addressed during the training. It will also help distinguish "need to know" from "nice to know." By focusing on what the trainees actually need to know in order to do their jobs better, a program can be developed that will get results.

To *Provide a Basis of Measurement* A needs assessment provides a baseline against which to measure results or changes. It is simply a starting point.

To *Gain Management Support* By involving line management and other key organizational players in the process, you will find the support you need for the training program to succeed. Because they have had input, they will have a vested interest in the program. Management commitment comes if managers and supervisors see that you are developing training programs in direct response to their specific needs.

NEEDS-ASSESSMENT PROCESS

The needs-assessment process can be as detailed and involved as needed or desired. Many factors must be taken into consideration, including time, money, number of people involved, resources available, and so forth.

A full-blown needs assessment is both time-consuming and costly. Frankly, few organizations are willing to make that kind of investment. A typical alternative is to conduct an abbreviated form of needs assessment, using only two or three methods.

Figure 1.1 offers a comparison between an in-depth and a mini needs assessment.

FIGURE 1.1. In-Depth versus Mini Needs Assessment

	In-Depth	Mini
Type of Information	Quantitative	Qualitative
Methods	Multi-tiered approach	Interviews
	Surveys	Focus groups
	Observation	
	Interviews	
	Focus groups	
	Document reviews	
Scope	Widespread organizational involvement	Fewer people involved
	Broad-ranging objectives	Short-term focus
Length	Several months to a year	Few days to a week
Cost	Expensive	Inexpensive
Focus	Linked to defined outputs	Immediate, quick results
	Long-term	
Exposure/Visibility	High profile and risk	Lower risk

Whom to Assess

The people assessed depends on the goal and the required depth of the assessment. Consider the following categories of people and then decide which groups to target as data sources.

Senior Management To get a clear picture of the problem and its business impact, start with senior management. Ask more strategic questions that address the direction of the organization as well as anticipated industry changes. In other words, start with an organizational context.

Here are some questions that will help you gain a better understanding of the organization's business needs:

- "What is the vision of the organization?"
- "What is the mission of the organization?"
- "What are the primary goals and objectives, both short-term and long-term?"
- "What organization or industry issues are driving the need for training?"
- "What is your most critical concern right now?"

Target Population It is also important to involve the target population, those who will receive the training. Often they are overlooked. They should be contacted to find out both their perceived and real training needs. If they are not consulted, it is unlikely that they will have a sense of ownership or "buy-in," and they will most likely approach the training experience with resistance and resentment.

Target Population's Managers Those who manage members of the target population are a critical source of data, since the purpose of the training is to help the line manager solve a business problem or meet a business need. These business needs may include improved productivity, decreased errors, fewer accidents, increased business, decreased turnover or absenteeism, or fewer customer complaints.

Direct Reports When the target population consists of managers or supervisors, good sources of data are those who report to these people. Direct reports can often provide valuable insight into the skills that managers and supervisors need to improve.

Co-Workers or Peers More and more organizations are using 360-degree feedback as part of the assessment process, providing employees with performance feedback from multiple sources. Talking with or surveying the target population's co-workers or peers, for example, can provide valuable insight into the skills necessary for a successful team environment. The more organizations that use cross-functional teams, the more critical the need becomes to involve other team members in the assessment process.

Human Resource Personnel The Human Resource (HR) Department is probably the best source of records and documents. They, of course, will have data on turnover, grievances, safety violations, and so forth, as well as performance appraisals and the like.

Vendors Vendors are a good source of qualitative data. They can share their perceptions of the organization or specific departments with which they interact, plus give some valuable insights into industry standards and practices.

Customers (Internal and External) Customer surveys provide quantitative data that can help pinpoint specific deficiencies, gaps between desired and actual behavior. Survey data will provide information on the level of satisfaction relative to customer-service practices, the quality of the product or service, and delivery systems.

Competitors Published competitor data such as sales results, market share, stock prices, and financial reports help to identify the organization's position in relation to its competitors and helps to pinpoint areas for improvement. Gather these data from an organization's annual report or from trade publications.

Industry Experts or Observers Industry experts have their thumbs on the pulse of the business in which an organization is engaged. They identify trends and industry standards against which an organization can measure itself. Experts may be identified through trade publications, where they may have written about the industry or may have been cited by others as experts in the field. One can also learn about and from experts by attending their sessions at professional conferences.

How to Conduct

Exhibit 1.1 provides an overview of the needs-assessment process.

Step One: Identify Problem or Need A good place to start is to take a look at the organization's statements of vision, mission, values, and goals. Ask to look at the strategic plan. If these organizational data do not exist, suggest that these statements and documents be developed before addressing any training issues. Because the purpose of training is to help solve organizational problems, you must have a clear understanding of what the business problems are.

The first step is to identify the problem or need, stated in dollar terms, if possible. Find out what the problem is costing the organization in errors, turnover, lost business, or additional help. Remember that the *desired outcome minus the current outcome is the need*.

After the need has been determined, define the specific objective the training program should meet. The objective must state the desired performance or

EXHIBIT 1.1. Needs-Assessment Process

Step One: Identify Problem or Need

- Determine organizational context
- Perform gap analysis
- Set objectives

Step Two: Determine Design of Needs Analysis

- Establish method-selection criteria
- Assess advantages and disadvantages of methods

Step Three: Collect Data

- Conduct interviews
- Administer questionnaires
- Administer surveys
- Review documents
- Observe people at work

Step Four: Analyze Data

- Conduct qualitative analysis
- Conduct quantitative analysis
- Determine solutions/recommendations

Step Five: Provide Feedback

- Write report
- Make oral presentation
- Determine next step

behavior and be measurable, observable, realistic, and "fixable." Working with line managers, determine what to measure and how to tie it to organizational goals. Outcomes relate to the specific need. For example, the goal or outcome of safety training is to reduce accidents by a particular percentage. Customer-service training should result in fewer customer complaints.

While examining possible causes, it is important to ask, "Is the problem due to a lack of knowledge or skill or is it operational?" For example, improper telephone use may have been identified as the problem. Incoming calls are being disconnected when the person who answers the call tries to transfer his or her calls. At first glance, it might appear that the people handling inbound calls need telephone skills training. However, if the telephone system is not set up to handle multiple functions, then training will not solve the problem.

Step Two: Determine Needs-Assessment Design To determine the true causes, not just the symptoms, of the problem or need, employ several investigative tools and techniques, including interviews, surveys, questionnaires, observation, and document examination. Choose investigative or data-collection methods on the basis of their appropriateness to the problem. The choice of methods will depend on various criteria, such as time, cost, or available resources. These criteria, as well as the advantages and disadvantages of various data-collection methods, will be explained later in Module One.

Step Three: Collect Data
Many methods are available for conducting a needs assessment, including

Data-Collection Methods and Tools

- Interviews
- Questionnaires
- Attitude surveys
- Observation
- Tests of proficiency
- Organizational statements and plans
- Turnover records
- Performance appraisals
- Procedures, handbooks, or audits
- Training evaluations
- Exit interviews
- Samples of work
- Job descriptions
- Complaints, error rates, and rejects
- Call reports, incident reports, and grievances
- Trade, government, and business publications

Criteria for Selecting a Method. From the rather extensive list of methods, select those most appropriate for the situation. Many factors will determine which methods to select. Look at the criteria in Exhibit 1.2, think about your own needs-assessment situation, and determine which criteria should be taken into consideration.

Advantages and Disadvantages of Methods. Data-collection methods fall roughly into six categories: open-ended questionnaires, closed-ended questionnaires, survey instruments, interviews, observation, and document examination.

EXHIBIT 1.2. Criteria for Selecting a Method

- Time
- Cost
- Number of people involved
- Workplace disruption
- Complexity
- Confidentiality
- Trust level
- Comfort level, knowledge, expertise of assessor
- Validity
- Reliability
- Adaptability
- Participant friendly

To help determine which data-collection methods to use, it is a good idea to look at the advantages and disadvantages of each, as shown in Figure 1.2. Weigh these considerations against your chosen criteria.

The most common approaches are covered in detail below.

Interviews. Whether for an in-depth or an abbreviated needs assessment, one-on-one and group interviews are valuable data sources. When developing interview questions, be sure to ask open-ended rather than closed-ended questions. Closed-ended questions can be answered with a simple "yes" or "no." For example, a question such as "Do you think there is a need for training?" elicits a one-word response. Probe further by asking an open-ended question. To get to the heart of the matter right away, ask a question that begins with "how" or "what" such as, "What would help you do your job better?" Try to avoid asking questions that begin with "why." First, people may not know why. Also, "why" questions tend to put people on the defensive.

Sample Interview Questions. Plan to take considerable time and care when writing questions. Not only should they be designed to elicit as much information as possible, but the questions must produce answers that will provide meaningful information. Although questions will vary according to the specific situation, some sample questions are included below that may help. After reading sample interview questions, make a list of questions you might ask. Be sure to identify your interviewees. Different questions are required for the employees in the target audience and for their managers.

Questions for Target Audience

- "What is a typical day for you?"
- "With whom do you interact on a regular basis?"

FIGURE 1.2. Advantages and Disadvantages of Data-Collection Methods

	Advantages	Disadvantages
Open-Ended Questionnaires	Allow respondent to introduce new topics Easy to develop Inexpensive to administer	Communication is one way Respondents may not want to put comments in writing Prone to ambiguity and opinions
Closed-Ended Questionnaires	Easier to answer Inexpensive to administer Feeling of anonymity and confidentiality ensured Less time consuming	Limited information Require more skill and work to prepare Items subject to misinterpretation Difficult and time consuming to construct
Instruments	Validated through research Quickly and easily administered Can be administered in groups Scored quickly	Administration and coordination needed Difficulty in choosing most appropriate Difficult and time consuming to construct Need to research different types
Individual or Group Interviews	Can read nonverbal messages Easier to talk Build commitment for training Clarifies expectations Can introduce now topics More detailed information	Time consuming Some people may feel threatened Can be affected by interviewer bias Difficult to organize and analyze data People may be influenced by peers
Observation	Better understanding of variables Provides real-life data and examples that can be used in course material Real situations, highly relevant Relatively low cost	Time consuming; expensive Requires some knowledge of the job People may be anxious, nervous Difficult to record data
Analysis of Existing Information	Factual, highly valid information Easy access to many sources in one place Inexpensive and not very time consuming Unobtrusive Provides specific examples	May be outdated May not cover all areas needed; too generic May be hard to find or access Risks misinterpretation May be biased

- "What are the typical situations, customers, or projects that you deal with?"
- "What training have you received to prepare you for your position?"
- "What additional training do you think you need to help you do your job better?"
- "What are the most difficult aspects of your job?"
- "What do you like best about your job?"
- "How do you know you are doing a good job?"
- "What type of feedback do you receive about your job performance?"
- "How often do you receive feedback?"

Questions for Managers of Target Audience

- "What would you like your employees to do differently?"
- "How would you describe the current level of performance in your department (or unit or team)?"
- "What are the important issues, problems, or changes your employees face at the present time?"
- "What skills, knowledge, or behaviors do you think your employees need to acquire or improve in order to do their jobs better?"
- "What are the potential barriers that might get in the way of your training efforts?"
- "What methods do you use to measure employee performance?"
- "How often do you give feedback to your employees about their performance?"
- "What is the biggest challenge you face as a manager?"

As mentioned earlier, communication is critical throughout the process. Interviews must be carefully planned and executed. The following guidelines will help you to conduct interviews smoothly and efficiently. The steps in the interview process are outlined below.

Schedule in Advance. Be respectful of people's time. Be sure to contact interviewees well in advance of the interview and arrange meetings at their convenience. If they view an interview as an imposition and a disruption, they will probably not be as forthcoming or cooperative in responding to questions. It is also helpful to send the questions in advance so that they can prepare or think about their answers. This preparation will enable the interview to move along more efficiently, and the interviewees' answers will be more meaningful.

Prepare Agenda. Good meeting management includes an agenda, prepared and sent out well in advance of the meeting. Needs-assessment interviews are no exception. Be sure to indicate the purpose and provide some direction or guidelines on how the interviewees can prepare for the interview.

Of course, also include logistical information such as the date, location, and the time (both starting and ending).

Ensure Privacy. This point should be a given; however, unless you take special care to arrange for a private meeting spot ahead of time, you might find yourself meeting in a less-than-ideal environment.

Eliminate Distractions and Interruptions. Once again, planning is key. Take the necessary steps to ensure there are no interruptions during the interview. In many cases, this means that you will need to communicate the importance of the interview session in advance and request the interviewee to do whatever it takes to maintain an interruption-free environment.

Clarify Purpose. Begin the interview by clarifying the purpose of the meeting. Emphasize the importance of the needs-assessment process and clearly explain the entire process and what will be done with the information. Give interviewees an opportunity to ask questions about the process before beginning the formal interview session.

Stress Confidentiality. Assure all interviewees that their answers and remarks will be held in the strictest confidence. Be sure to explain how the information will be used. Focus groups, in particular, need to be reminded that, although the speaker's identity will be protected, what the person says will be recorded. It is critical that members of the focus group respect one another and not divulge any information shared within the group.

Some helpful hints for interviewing techniques are given below:

Use Good Communication Techniques. To be an effective interviewer, hone your active listening skills, particularly your ability to clarify and confirm. Interviewees are prone to rambling and talking in generalities. Make sure that you understand clearly what the other person is saying. The following clarifying and confirming techniques will help to gather the needed information:

- "Tell me more about . . . ."
- "Give me an example of . . . ."
- "Let me make sure I understand. What I heard was . . . ."
- "If I heard you correctly, you believe that . . . ."

Whatever you do, do not say, "What you mean is . . ." or "What you're saying is . . . ." These statements imply that the speaker is not articulate enough to express himself or herself, and you have to help him or her out.

Observation. Observation involves a trained person observing others on the job. Observations are often used to validate information gathered by other methods such as interviews or questionnaires. Another observation technique makes use of an outside "shopper." Some organizations (banks, retail sales) hire outside professionals to conduct telephone or face-to-face shopping surveys. With this method, representatives from the consulting company go into a store or branch office and pretend to be customers. They note specific behaviors, such as how they were greeted, friendliness, and knowledge level of the employees. They may look for evidence of cross-selling efforts or an offer of further assistance.

Questionnaires and Survey Instruments. An important consideration in using instruments is whether to develop them or purchase them. Questionnaires with open-ended questions are easy to construct, whereas questionnaires with closed-ended questions require more time and thought. Although published surveys can be costly, using them can not only save time, but will yield more accurate information because they have been tested for validity and reliability. Be aware, however, that published instruments may or may not be specific enough for a particular situation. For both questionnaires and surveys, be sure to send a cover letter to participants explaining the purpose and what will be done with the results of the instrument. Make the instructions crystal clear.

Step Four: Analyze Data Data analysis can be simple or quite complex, depending on the methods chosen. For qualitative data, such as individual or group interviews, as well as for open-ended questionnaires and observation, do a content analysis, sorting information into categories (for example, positive and negative reactions) and identifying common themes. The goal of the content analysis is to categorize and quantify the data as much as possible with minimal interpretation.

For quantitative data (survey instruments and closed-ended questionnaires), do a statistical analysis. Keep it as simple as possible. Do not become engulfed in number-crunching activities. Look at the data in terms of mean (the average, calculated by adding all the values and dividing by the number in the group), mode (the number that occurs most frequently), and median (the middle number in a numerical listing).

If your research indicates that training is appropriate, specify the type of training called for. Should it be workshop training, on-the-job, self-study, or what? Training must address the problem specifically, and the systems must be in place to support the training outcomes. For example, you may identify a customer-service training program as the solution to customer complaints and lost business. Participants in the training will learn how to handle customer complaints tactfully and respond to customer inquiries politely and efficiently. Yet the program will fail if slow delivery makes it hard for the customer to buy the product.

Clarify and Define the Problem. Although the problem may have been stated at the beginning of the needs-assessment process by the key players in the organization, those are really *perceptions* of the problem. The data-collection process and subsequent analysis of that data will help to clarify and to define the *real* problem.

NEEDS-ASSESSMENT EXAMPLE

A client once asked me to deliver a stress management program for a group of executive secretaries. In a discussion with my contact, the training director, I probed to uncover what events may have triggered the request. During a recent company-wide employee meeting, several secretaries were quite outspoken in expressing their dissatisfaction with the way they were being treated. As a result, senior management concluded that this group needed stress management. Although actual performance had not been affected, the morale and interpersonal relationships were deteriorating rapidly. I suggested that before I developed a program specific to their situation, it would be a good idea to talk with a few of the members of the target audience. The training director agreed, and we arranged a focus group meeting with six of the secretaries. As I listened to the secretaries, it became increasingly clear that most of the stress the secretaries were experiencing stemmed from a single cause: the inability of the secretaries and managers to communicate effectively with one another. After listening to the secretaries' complaints and perceptions of the problem, I concluded that a stress management program was not the answer. In fact, it would be a waste of time and money. I suggested that we attack the cause of the problem, not its symptoms. I recommended that I design and deliver a program that would promote open, two-way communication between each secretary and his or her immediate supervisor by showing them how to improve their communication skills and to work more effectively as members of a boss/secretary team.

During the analysis phase, you will add to your perceptions of the problem through qualitative data such as interviews and focus groups. Verify your perceptions with survey results and other quantitative data. After categorizing the data, the next step is to identify priorities, always keeping in mind the business need. The prioritization process is extremely important because the needs assessment will probably result in a long list of training needs. Based on an analysis of the data, make your recommendations for specific training programs or interventions.

Step Five: Provide Feedback After the data have been collected and analyzed, identify the area(s) of need, design an action plan or strategies, and communicate your conclusions and recommendations to key personnel. This feedback should be delivered in both a written and an oral format. As you prepare to communicate your findings and recommendations, keep in mind that the goal is to obtain approval for your proposal. Plan a strategy for presenting the information in a positive light. Carefully think through what (and how much) to share, how to share, and with whom to share findings and recommendations.

The Written Report. The final report is a critical piece. It should be constructed in such a way that it presents the data in an easy-to-understand format, along with conclusions and recommendations. The length of the final report, of course, depends on how extensive the assessment is. In any case, the written report should contain the following elements:

- *Executive Overview.* Provide an overview of the proposal for executives, an abbreviated, concise representation of the larger document, limited to one page, and distributed to the key decision makers.
- *Description of the Process.* Provide appropriate background information, such as the problem statement or current situation, and briefly describe the entire needs-assessment process, including purpose, scope, methods used, and the people involved. Be sure to include your rationale, that is, your reason for conducting a needs assessment.
- *Summary of Findings.* In this section, present data clearly and concisely, highlighting patterns or significant results.
- *Preliminary Conclusions.* Address the analysis of the data, focusing on key issues that have surfaced. It may be appropriate to show how the findings relate to or support your (or others') perceptions. Point out how the issues relate to the business need. Do not assume that readers will make the connection by themselves.
- *Recommendations.* At this point, list your ideas and recommended solutions to the problem. When identifying training issues, be clear about what programs should be implemented, who should be involved, and how, when, and where the training will take place. Be careful not to lock yourself in by being too specific.
- *Potential Barriers.* Solutions to problems are not without problems themselves. Take a proactive approach by addressing potential barriers up-front and suggesting ways to overcome them. Potential barriers can be almost anything, but the most common will probably be cost, time commitment, and the commitment of the target audience and/or their managers.

Oral Presentation. In addition to the written proposal, plan to present your information and recommendations to a selected audience. The oral presentation is an opportunity to hear reactions from the key players. Be prepared for questions and challenges. Anticipate what they may be and have responses and answers ready. Look at the presentation as a chance to sell your ideas. That means you will need to fine-tune your persuasion and influencing skills. Ask someone who is a skillful presenter and persuader to coach you before your presentation, or if you have the time and the opportunity, participate in a workshop on persuasive presentations.

Selected Audience. The selected audience depends on a number of factors, such as the corporate culture and internal politics. In general, include key decision makers and representative stakeholders, such as members of the target audience, their managers, and anyone who may have a vested interest in the program's success. Also, the number of meetings and the organizational levels involved in receiving the feedback should relate to the scope of the assessment. For example, if everyone in the organization completed an employee-opinion survey, then every employee should receive feedback.

Length. In many cases, you may have little control over the length of the presentation. Senior management will probably determine the time available based on their schedules, priorities, and other commitments. If they do not, then request an hour. That will give enough time to present your case and address any questions or concerns the executives might raise.

Format/Approach. The key is to present findings in summary form. Use transparencies of bulleted points and simple charts and graphs to illustrate and highlight important information.

DEVELOPING AN ACTION PLAN

After presenting the information and making recommendations, solicit reactions and feedback from the key players. It is possible that they will immediately approve your proposal. More likely, however, you will be asked to make some modifications. In some cases, you may have to go back to the drawing board several times.

After your proposal has been approved, map out a plan for the design, development, and delivery of the program(s). Include specific action items with a time line and appropriate task assignments.

The next step in the process of designing a program to meet the specific developmental needs of the participants and the business needs of the organization is to write learning outcomes or objectives, which are addressed in detail in Module Five. However, before you begin the design and development process, examine some critical elements that are often overlooked: how adults learn; the different learning styles of your participants; and your own training style. Finally, examine some of the diversity issues in today's workplace that will have an impact on how you design, develop, and deliver effective training programs. These important considerations are addressed in Modules Two, Three, and Four.

ASSESSING PARTICIPANTS' KNOWLEDGE, ATTITUDES, AND SKILLS

So far, we have looked at the needs-assessment process that serves as the basis of training design, development, and evaluation. It may seem that after you receive the go-ahead to design and develop a program targeted to specific needs, the needs-assessment task is over. Not so! You also must assess the knowledge, attitudes, and skill level of the participants prior to each session. Different audiences may have different needs.

Pre-Session Questionnaire

A short, simple, and straightforward questionnaire such as the one shown in Exhibit 1.3 can be an invaluable tool in fine-tuning your program. The information you receive from such a questionnaire will help you in many ways:

1. It can help to design the program at the appropriate level, not insulting participants' intelligence (and boring them to death) by dealing with content they already know. By the same token, you do not want to lose them by talking over their heads.

2. A questionnaire allows you to identify those participants who have greater familiarity with the training topic so that you can draw on them as resources. Conversely, by identifying those with less familiarity with a topic, you know who may need additional attention or encouragement.

3. The questionnaire will help to weed out those who do not belong in the session because they are underqualified, overqualified, or doing work for which the program is irrelevant. This is particularly important for voluntary, open-enrollment programs advertised to all employees in an organization. Unfortunately, no matter how well the course description identifies the target audience and learning outcomes, invariably those who do not read beyond the title will sign up for programs for which they are not suited. When that happens, take the person aside, explain that the session may not meet his or her expectations, and offer the person the option of leaving. Should the person choose to stay, you have at least been up-front about what the participant can and cannot expect.

4. The questionnaire can be used to gather information to use in creating real-life case studies, skill practice, and examples. The more relevant the material, the more the participants will embrace the training. Of course, assure the participants that their contributions may be used but not identified.

5. The questionnaire can identify potential problems caused by negative attitudes so that you can take steps to overcome these barriers or pockets of resistance.

6. The questionnaire can create a positive learning environment even before the program starts. It can help participants be mentally prepared for the training. Also, your interest in them even before they come to your session will make them more receptive to you and what you have to offer.

EXHIBIT 1.3.
Confidential Pre-Session
Questionnaire

MANAGEMENT SKILLS AND TECHNIQUES PART III

The purpose of this questionnaire is to provide the facilitator of this program with insights into your current skills in or knowledge about the subject of managing others. By knowing what new skills and knowledge you would like from the program, the facilitator will be better able to meet your needs.

Name: _____   Current Position: _____

Bank: _____   City, State: _____

Previous positions held:

Formal education beyond high school:

What management courses, workshops, or seminars have you attended?

Briefly describe the responsibilities of your current position:

How long have you managed or supervised others?

How many people do you directly supervise or manage?

What do you believe is the most difficult problem or challenge you face in managing people?

What one specific thing do you want to learn from this program?

What concerns do you have about participating in this learning experience?

On-the-Spot Assessment

Regardless of how extensive your needs assessment is, it is also a good idea to conduct an informal, on-the-spot, individual needs assessment at the beginning of the first session. Start by asking the participants what they expect from the session. Their answers will give an indication of whether or not your design is on target. This on-the-spot assessment will also provide an opportunity to clarify participants' expectations. Reinforce those expectations that are on target with the training design or make last-minute adjustments to the program, to make sure that participants' needs are met. Sometimes, participants may have expectations that you cannot possibly meet in the session. Module Eight covers some specific interactive on-the-spot needs-assessment activities.

✦ ✦ ✦

Module Two

Understanding Adult Learners

LEARNING OUTCOMES

In this module, you will

- Examine the basic principles of adult learning that all trainers should know
- Identify ways to overcome resistance to learning
- Define your own role in the success of the training experience

---

TRAINER CHARACTERISTICS AND COMPETENCIES

Recall your *best* and *worst* learning experiences from any time in your life (elementary school, high school, college, organizations, work). For each experience, briefly describe the highlights and list what factors made that experience good or bad.

Description of Good Experience:

Factors That Made It Good:

Description of Bad Experience:

Factors That Made It Bad:

Think about your feelings and reactions to both the good and bad experiences. How effective was the learning experience? To what degree did the training or learning experience contribute to your success?

During discussions of these questions in train-the-trainer programs, participants are quick to respond that the single most important factor in the success or failure of the learning experience was the instructor. People often share that the positive experiences had a positive impact on their success in life and that the negative experiences created major obstacles to further education and training. In some cases, the negative experiences prevented them from seeking or taking advantage of opportunities that could have led to career advancement.

Are You Trainer Material?

Being good at your job does not guarantee that you will be good at training someone else how to do it. To be effective, trainers must perfect their competencies in the following areas:

- First and foremost, training professionals must have a business orientation. They must concern themselves with improving performance and focus on business outcomes.
- Training professionals must also be able to recognize and admit when training is not the appropriate solution for a problem.
- To succeed in a diverse environment, trainers must fine-tune their interpersonal skills and be able to adapt to a variety of people, cultures, and situations.
- Those responsible for training others in a workshop setting must develop and master training skills. True professionals spend their entire lives honing their craft and perfecting their skills, learning new skills, and keeping up-to-date on the latest trends, concepts, and applications in the field.

Over the years, educational research has identified personal and professional characteristics or attributes that are associated with successful teachers. These same attributes can be ascribed to trainers as well. Review the checklist in Exhibit 2.1 to identify those characteristics you bring to your role as a trainer. Place a check mark next to those that describe you.

Andragogical versus Pedagogical Model

People have been "brought up" on the pedagogical model of learning that has dominated education and training for centuries. Because that has been the

EXHIBIT 2.1.
Characteristics of
Effective Trainers

___	Knowledge of subject	___	Empathetic; understanding
___	Genuine	___	Sense of humor
___	Well organized	___	Uses a variety of methods
___	Goal oriented	___	Warm; approachable
___	Strong presence; poise	___	Tactful
___	Professional appearance	___	Good voice quality
___	Ability to relate content to participants' situations	___	Enthusiastic
___	Patient	___	Good listener
___	Flexible; spontaneous	___	Positive self-concept
___	Positive attitude	___	Honest and open
___	Credible	___	Participant centered
___	Ability to relate to others at all levels	___	Respectful of participants
___	Objective	___	Emotional stability
		___	Diagnostician
		___	Coach and counselor
		___	Articulate

standard, people use that approach when they are asked to teach or train others. In brief, the pedagogical model makes the following assumptions:

- The teacher is responsible for the learning process, including what and how learners learn. The learner's role is passive.
- Because the learner has little experience, the teacher is the expert, the guru, and it is his or her responsibility to impart his or her wealth of knowledge. This amounts to an "information dump" through traditional means such as lecture, textbooks, manuals, and videos in which other "experts" share their knowledge and experience.
- People are motivated to learn because "they have to" in order to pass a test, advance to the next level, or earn certification.
- Learning is information-centered. The teacher "covers the material" so that the learner can acquire the prescribed information in some type of logical order.
- Motivation to learn is largely external. Pressure from authority figures and fear of negative consequences drive the learner. The teacher, in essence, controls the learning through rewards and discipline.

UNDERSTANDING HOW AND WHY PEOPLE LEARN

Although adult education theorists differ on just how different adults are from children, most embrace the andragogical theory of adult learning. During the 1960s, European adult educators coined the term "andragogy" to provide a label for a growing body of knowledge and technology in regard to adult learning. The concept was introduced and advanced in the United States by Malcolm Knowles. The following assumptions underlie the andragogical model of learning, which Knowles now calls a model of human learning (Knowles, 1990).

Assumption One

The first assumption involves a change in self-concept from total dependency to increasing *self-directedness*. The adult learner is self-directed. Adult learners want to take responsibility for their own lives, including planning, implementing, and evaluating their learning activities. This principle is often misinterpreted. Learner self-directedness does not mean that the trainer abdicates responsibility for the plan or approach. From the beginning, the trainer establishes the training process as a collaborative effort. Throughout the process, the trainer and participant are partners engaged in ongoing, two-way communication.

Assumption Two

The second principle addresses the role of *experience*, a principle unique to the adult learner. According to Knowles, each of us brings to a learning situation a wealth of experiences that provide a basis for new learning as well as a resource to share with others. These experiences may be good or bad, but they will impact the way in which an employee approaches a new learning experience. Because people base their learning on past experiences, the new information must be assimilated. The wise trainer will find out what the participants already know and will build on those experiences, rather than treating participants as though they know nothing and must be taught like small children.

Assumption Three

The third assumption is that adults are ready to learn when they perceive a *need to know or do something* in order to perform more effectively in some aspect of their lives. The days of abstract theories and concepts are over for most adults. They want the learning experience to be practical and realistic, problem-centered rather than subject-centered. The effective trainer helps participants understand how learning a particular skill or task will help them be more successful, that is, how the employee can do the job more quickly, easily, or efficiently.

Assumption Four

Fourth, adults want immediate, *real-world applications*. They want the skills and knowledge to help them solve problems or complete tasks. People are motivated to learn when they see relevance to their real lives and are able to apply what they have learned as quickly as possible. Therefore, learning activities must be clearly relevant to the immediate needs of the adult. To be effective, deliver just-in-time training and emphasize how the training is going to make participants' jobs easier.

Assumption Five

Finally, adults are motivated to learn because of *internal factors* such as self-esteem, desire for recognition, natural curiosity, innate love of learning, better quality of life, greater self-confidence or the opportunity to self-actualize.

Principles of Adult Learning

As you begin to design and develop any training program for adults, keep in mind these additional principles regarding how people learn:

Learning Styles   People learn through a variety of ways. One person may learn better by listening; another may be visual or may prefer to read instructions. Someone else may need a demonstration. Learning style refers to the way in which a learner approaches and responds to a learning experience. There are several learning style assessments available on the market, including the following instruments, published in the Jossey-Bass/Pfeiffer *Annuals*:

- *Learning-Style Inventory* by Ronne Toker Jacobs and Barbara Schneider Fuhrmann (1984)
- *The Learning-Model Instrument* by Kenneth L. Murrell (1987)
- *The Dunn and Dunn Model of Learning Styles* by Joanne Ingham and Rita Dunn (1993)

David Kolb's *Learning Style Inventory* (1981) is used widely as a basis for other models and instruments. These, among others, are all excellent tools to help identify learning style. The self-assessment process heightens one's awareness that different people learn in different ways and sensitizes people to the importance of designing training that addresses all learning styles.

Determining Your Learning Style To get a flavor for style differences and to further your understanding of your preferred learning style, complete the learning style assessment in Exhibit 2.2, then score and study it.

Keep in mind that no one learning style is right or even better than another. The point is that each person learns differently. A variety of learning styles will be represented in any training session. To be effective, trainers must design their programs to accommodate style differences. Predictably, trainers often use only the style they prefer. Although it is natural to use the style with which one is most comfortable, the most effective trainers know how to adapt their styles to meet the needs of all participants. You will have an opportunity to find out about your preferred training style in Module Three.

Perceptual Modality In addition to learning styles, an effective trainer must be able to understand the different perceptual modalities. According to M.B. James and M.W. Galbraith (1985), a learner may prefer one of the following six perceptual modalities, ways in which one takes in and processes information:

Visual	Videos; slides; graphs; photos; demonstrations; methods and media that create opportunities for the participant to experience learning through the eyes
Print	Texts; paper-and-pencil exercises that enable the participant to absorb the written word
Aural	Lectures; audiotapes; methods that allow the participant to simply listen and take in information through the ears
Interactive	Group discussions; question-and-answer sessions; ways that give the participant an opportunity to talk and engage in an exchange of ideas, opinions, and reactions with fellow participants
Tactile	Hands-on activities; model building; methods that require the participant to handle objects or put things together
Kinesthetic	Role plays; physical games and activities; ways that involve the use of psychomotor skills and movement from one place to another

EXHIBIT 2.2. Learning Style Profile

Instructions: For each of the numbered items below, rank alternatives A through D by assigning 4 to the phrase that is most like you, 3 to the one that next describes you, 2 to the next, and finally, 1 to the ending that is least descriptive of you.

1. When solving a problem, I prefer to

   a. take a step-by-step approach
   b. take immediate action
   c. consider the impact on others
   d. make sure I have all the facts

2. As a learner, I prefer to

   a. listen to a lecture
   b. work in small groups
   c. read articles and case studies
   d. participate in role plays

3. When the trainer asks a question to which I know the answer, I

   a. let others answer first
   b. offer an immediate response
   c. consider whether my answer will be received favorably
   d. think carefully about my answer before responding

4. In a group discussion, I

   a. encourage others to offer their opinions
   b. question others' opinions
   c. readily offer my opinion
   d. listen to others before offering my opinion

5. I learn best from activities in which I

   a. can interact with others
   b. remain uninvolved
   c. take a leadership role
   d. can take my time

6. During a lecture, I listen for

   a. practical how-to's
   b. logical points
   c. the main idea
   d. stories and anecdotes

EXHIBIT 2.2.
Continued

7. I am impressed by a trainer's

    a. knowledge and expertise
    b. personality and style
    c. use of methods and activities
    d. organization and control

8. I prefer information to be presented in the following way:

    a. model such as a flow chart
    b. bullet points
    c. detailed explanation
    d. accompanied by examples

9. I learn best when I

    a. see relationships between ideas, events, and situations
    b. interact with others
    c. receive practical tips
    d. observe a demonstration or video

10. Before attending a training program, I ask myself, "Will I . . . ?"

    a. get practical tips to help me in my job
    b. receive lots of information
    c. have to participate
    d. learn something new

11. After attending a training session, I

    a. tend to think about what I learned
    b. am anxious to put my learning into action
    c. reflect on the experience as a whole
    d. tell others about my experience

12. The training method I dislike the most is

    a. participating in small groups
    b. listening to a lecture
    c. reading and analyzing case studies
    d. participating in role plays

EXHIBIT 2.2.
Continued

Scoring Sheet

Instructions: Record your responses on the appropriate spaces below, then total the columns.

Feelers	*Observers*	*Thinkers*	*Doers*
1c___	1a___	1d___	1b___
2b___	2a___	2c___	2d___
3c___	3a___	3d___	3b___
4a___	4d___	4b___	4c___
5a___	5b___	5d___	5c___
6d___	6c___	6b___	6a___
7b___	7d___	7a___	7c___
8d___	8a___	8c___	8b___
9b___	9d___	9a___	9c___
10d___	10c___	10b___	10a___
11d___	11c___	11a___	11b___
12c___	12a___	12d___	12b___

Totals   ___   ___   ___   ___

Interpretation of Scores

Feelers. Feelers are very people-oriented. They are expressive and focus on feelings and emotions. They enjoy affective learning and gravitate toward learning experiences that explore people's attitudes and emotions. Feelers thrive in an open, unstructured learning environment. They appreciate the opportunity to work in groups and like activities where they can share opinions and experiences.

Observers. Observers like to watch and listen. They tend to be reserved and quiet and will take their time before acting or participating in class. When they do decline to offer an opinion or answer a question, they are generally right on target. They enjoy learning experiences that allow them to consider various ideas and opinions, and they seem to thrive on learning though discovery.

EXHIBIT 2.2.
Continued

Thinkers. Thinkers rely on logic and reason. They like the opportunity to share ideas and concepts. They prefer activities that require them to analyze and evaluate. They will question the rationale behind activities and will challenge statements that they perceive to be too general or without substance. Thinkers prefer to work independently and question the relevance of role plays and simulations.

Doers. Doers like to be actively involved in the learning process. They will take charge in group activities and tend to dominate discussions. They like opportunities to practice what they learn, and they are particularly interested in knowing how they are going to apply what they learn in the real world. They like information presented clearly and concisely, and they become impatient with drawn out discussions.

Research indicates that more adults are visual learners than any other perceptual style; however, a good training design incorporates all six modalities to ensure that all participants' needs are being addressed. Vary activities to create multi-sensory learning that will increase the likelihood of appealing to each participant's preferred style. A multi-sensory approach also helps each participant reinforce the knowledge or skills acquired through the preferred modality.

Learning should be presented in a way that complements each person's preferred style. For example, let's look at a design for training several people in a group setting to use a personal computer. The trainer includes pictures of the computer screen, illustrating what the person should see when he or she strikes a particular key. The trainer also demonstrates how to perform certain functions on the computer (*visual*). The training design includes print materials, such as a manual and short application-oriented quizzes (*print*). For review and reinforcement, the trainer prepares an audiotape (*aural*). During daily instructional sessions, the trainer provides many opportunities for the trainee to answer as well as ask questions (*interactive*). Of course, the design includes multiple opportunities for hands-on practice (*tactile*). Finally, the trainer creates simulation activities in which the participants will be asked to create "real-life" work-related documents such as spreadsheets, reports, or graphs (*kinesthetic*).

Another important consideration is that people generally learn by doing, not by being told how to do something. For example, a person learns more quickly how to reach a new location by driving the car rather than by observing as a passenger. The more opportunities a person has to "try out" or apply the skills, the more likely he or she is to learn the skills.

Telling is not teaching or training. How many times have you said to yourself, "I've told him and told him how to do it, but he still does it wrong"? Just because you tell someone how to do something does not mean that he or she understands it or has developed the skill to do it.

Still other factors affect the speed at which people learn.

Psychological Some people prefer the "big picture," while others want a step-by-step process.

Environmental Sound, light, temperature, and seating can all impact learning. For example, sitting in a hard chair for several hours will put stress on the body, interfering with a person's ability to concentrate.

Emotional Participants' motivation for attending the session will influence the learning process. Those who attend because they want to are more likely to have a positive learning experience than those who are there because their supervisors required them to attend.

Sociological People are by nature social beings. Although some people do learn better alone, studies show that most people learn better and experience greater satisfaction with the learning experience when they are in pairs or small groups.

Physical People's physical condition, including hearing, sight, general health, and energy level, impacts their ability to learn. Most people have less energy in the afternoon. Trainers must keep this in mind when designing and developing their programs.

Intellectual and Experiential People in sessions vary greatly in educational background, life experiences, innate intelligence, and abilities. That is why it is important to find out as much as possible about participants before they attend training sessions.

Age One of the frequent issues that comes up in train-the-trainer and coaching courses relates to the impact of age on the learning process. Managers, supervisors, and trainers often say that older workers are slower and more difficult to train. To set the record straight, researchers are somewhat divided on the issue of age and one's ability to learn, depending on one's interpretation of learning. In general, research on adult learning shows that adults continue to learn throughout the years; however, they may take longer to learn new things. Although younger people seem to be more efficient when it comes to memorizing information, older people are better able to evaluate and apply information. Research findings show that change in adulthood is a procession of critical periods during the fifty plus years following childhood and youth. These periods consist of marked changes and experiences during which some of the most meaningful learning may occur.

Adults have a potential for continuing learning and inquiry that conventional wisdom has sometimes failed to recognize. Researchers, however, do recognize that physical changes play a part in the learning process. As we age, we may experience some hearing loss, lower energy levels, and slower reaction times. These factors should be taken into consideration; however, they should not be regarded as proof that older people are slower or have greater difficulty learning. By observing adult-learning principles as well as basic concepts of individual differences and accommodating them accordingly, a trainer can effectively train any adult.

Cognitive Overload

Our minds are like sponges as we soak up knowledge and information. When sponges are saturated, any additional water will run right through. Just as the sponge can become overloaded, a learner can experience cognitive overload of his or her working memory. The working memory—the center of conscious thinking—has an estimated limited capacity of seven "chunks" or pieces of information. The limits of our working memory depend on the knowledge stored in long-term memory. A person who is quite comfortable with and knowledgeable about a subject can easily overwhelm those who are less familiar with the information. The challenge to the trainer is to present information in such a way that the participants do not experience overload.

Preventing Cognitive Overload

To prevent cognitive overload, use the following strategies when designing, developing, and delivering training:

- *Minimize the use of lecture.* Boil down information into key learning points, checklists, charts, graphs, or other visuals.
- *Have the participants do most of the work.* When the participants do the work, they transfer new information into long-term memory, much like storing data in a computer. The working memory is now free to absorb the next chunk of information.
- *Create chunks of content or information and distribute or communicate it incrementally.* Use a variety of activities to communicate the material.

> • *Design workbooks and other participant materials that present informa-tion in an easy-to-follow and easy-to-understand format.*
> • *Create job aids for use during and after the training.*

APPLICATION OF LEARNING PRINCIPLES

These concepts have certain implications for the trainer. The traditional or pedagogical orientation is concerned with content. Trainers are concerned with "covering" material in the most efficient way possible. In contrast, the andragogical orientation focuses on process, being attentive to the factors that either promote or inhibit learning.

Based on what you know about the adult learner and how learning takes place, take those principles and concepts and translate them into practical applications for your training programs. Consider the following points as you create a learning experience for your participants:

- Create a comfortable, nonthreatening learning climate in which people are treated as responsible adults.
- Involve participants in planning their training through interviews, advisory committees, and other up-front activities.
- Allow participants to engage in self-diagnosis by using questionnaires and assessment instruments both before and during sessions.
- Give participants an opportunity to set their own objectives by soliciting their input through pre-session questionnaires and assessment activities at the beginning of sessions.
- Give them an opportunity to evaluate their own learning through a variety of activities throughout the training program.
- Help participants to see how the training will help them.
- Make the learning relevant to participants by understanding and connecting with their frames of reference.
- Use their experiences by asking them to share examples from their own situations.
- Actively involve the participants in the learning process by using learner-centered activities and structured experiences and by providing them with many opportunities to master the content.

The more you understand about how and why adults learn, the better equipped you will be to design training programs that meet participants' needs and obtain the results you want.

◆   ◆   ◆

Module Three

Training Style

LEARNING OUTCOMES

In this module, you will learn

- To identify your own training-style preference
- To identify ways to increase your style flexibility

TRAINING STYLE

Even if you have never done any formal training or teaching, you have already developed a training style, a combination of training philosophies, methods, and behaviors, as the result of the experiences you have had as a learner and as an unofficial trainer. The way in which you give directions to others (co-workers, friends, family members), present information, or explain how to do something reflects a preferred training style.

Style Flexibility

Just as you have a preferred style of learning, you have a preferred approach for presenting content and relating to participants. Although you may have a strong preference for one style over another, you can and should learn to use the entire range of styles to connect with participants and facilitate the learning process.

Much like management or leadership styles, inherent in training styles is the need to balance continually concern for task or content with concern for people. This is further complicated by the fact that different training styles impact different types of learners in different ways.

Identifying Training Style

To heighten your awareness of your style preferences, complete the assessment instrument in Exhibit 3.1.

EXHIBIT 3.1.
Instructional Styles
Diagnosis Inventory, *Greg
Cripple**

Instructions: Think of your most recent learning experience with the trainer who is being evaluated. Each of the twenty items that follows contains four statements about what instructors can do or ways in which they can act.

Rank each set of statements to reflect the degree to which each statement in the set describes the trainer's instructional style. Assign a ranking of four (4) to the statement most characteristic or descriptive of the trainer; assign a three (3) to the next most descriptive statement; a two (2) to the next most descriptive statement; and a one (1) to the statement that is least descriptive of the trainer. Record your response for each statement in the blank next to it.

For some items, you may think that all statements are very descriptive or that none fit very well. To give the most accurate feedback, force yourself to rank the statements as best you can.

"WHEN INSTRUCTING ADULTS, THIS PERSON WOULD BE MOST LIKELY TO . . ."

1. ___ a. Allow extended practice or discussion in areas of particular interest to learners.
   ___ b. Judge trainer's effectiveness by how well the prepared materials are covered.
   ___ c. Sit down with learners while instructing them.
   ___ d. Set trainer up as a role model and encourage learners to emulate trainer.

2. ___ a. End a training session by summarizing the key subject matter and recommending that learners find ways to apply it on the job.
   ___ b. Arrange the room so as to provide for better discipline and control.
   ___ c. Use specific course objectives to inform learners as to what they should expect to be able to do.
   ___ d. Focus learners' attention more on themselves and their own performance than on trainer.

3. ___ a. Gain supervisors involvement by providing ideas on how to support learners' attempts to apply new skills.
   ___ b. Let the group "handle" difficult learners or privately explore reasons for problems.
   ___ c. Evaluate learners by giving examinations to test their retention of presented materials.
   ___ d. Carefully lead and control any group discussions.

Source: G. Cripple, Instructional-Styles Diagnosis Inventory: Increasing Style Awareness and Flexibility, in J.W. Pfeiffer, ed., *The 1996 Annual: Volume 1, Training.* San Francisco: Jossey-Bass/Pfeiffer.

EXHIBIT 3.1. *Continued*

4. ___ a. Put his or her primary focus on giving a technically polished presentation.

___ b. Avoid reducing impact by not disclosing any course materials prior to the program.

___ c. Show willingness to learn from learners by admitting errors or lack of knowledge when appropriate.

___ d. Collect background information and adjust the level of content material for each particular group.

5. ___ a. Involve learners in activities designed to stimulate critical or reflective thought.

___ b. Communicate positive expectations to slower learners through feedback and encouragement, in order to help them improve.

___ c. Motivate learners with enthusiastic talks, humorous stories, and entertaining or inspirational videos.

___ d. Maintain punctuality of published program schedules.

6. ___ a. Make occasional use of media tools to support other primary learning activities.

___ b. Present materials in the most logical order.

___ c. Allow learners to influence or prioritize course content and objectives.

___ d. Ensure that learners perform and apply newly learned skills as instructed.

7. ___ a. Thoroughly cover all subject-matter areas in the scheduled time allotted.

___ b. Change course materials or training methods based on feedback about learners' performance changes after training.

___ c. Maintain a consistent pace of presentation throughout the program.

___ d. Express concern for and interest in individual learners and their problems.

8. ___ a. Judge trainer's effectiveness based on learners' "liking" of trainer.

___ b. Allow learners to make mistakes and learn from session experiences.

___ c. Expose learners to traditionally accepted subject matter and correct procedures.

___ d. Ask learners questions designed to guide them to self-discovery of key points.

EXHIBIT 3.1. *Continued*

9.___ a. Frequently assess learners' body language and emotional states and adjust activities or schedule appropriately.

___ b. Explore content-related controversial issues as potential learning experiences.

___ c. Plan and structure course materials in considerable detail.

___ d. Begin program by informing learners of trainer's experience or qualifications and trainer's goals for the program.

10.___ a. Cite a bibliography of resources concerning materials discussed for further learner self-development.

___ b. Use position as instructor to quickly resolve "difficult learner" problems (e.g., monopolizers, side conversations, sharpshooters, etc.).

___ c. Encourage casual or comfortable dress to increase the informality of the learning environment.

___ d. Avoid potentially time-wasting tangents by dealing with learners' questions quickly and moving on.

11.___ a. Direct learners' attention primarily to trainer and to what is being said or demonstrated.

___ b. Frequently redirect learners' questions to other learners to be answered.

___ c. Send out self-study "prework" materials to spark learner interest and formation of course expectations.

___ d. Consistently cover the same material with each group.

12.___ a. Arrange the room so as to promote group activities and discussions.

___ b. Always stand in front of the class while instructing.

___ c. Send learners' bosses an overview of course subject matter.

___ d. Judge trainer's effectiveness based on how proficient learners are in performing new skills or applying new concepts on the job.

13.___ a. Project a professional image by maintaining a separation between trainer and learners.

___ b. Help learners motivate themselves by developing new skills through involvement and participation.

___ c. Closely direct learners' activities.

___ d. Allow learners to analyze materials and draw their own conclusions.

EXHIBIT 3.1. *Continued*

14. ___ a. End a training session by helping learners create action plans to apply course content to real-world problems.
___ b. Criticize slow learners to help them improve.
___ c. Avoid controversy as a potential distraction or turnoff.
___ d. Coach learners as they practice new skills.

15. ___ a. Encourage detailed note taking by learners.
___ b. Encourage learners to challenge outdated course materials or concepts of questionable value on the job.
___ c. Sequence activities so as to stimulate and hold learner interest.
___ d. Use media (video, slides, overheads, etc.) extensively to increase the professionalism of the presentation.

16. ___ a. Use an introductory overview to inform learners of the subject matter to be covered.
___ b. Judge trainer's effectiveness based on learners' increase in confidence and self-esteem.
___ c. Maintain a formal dress code to establish a more serious atmosphere.
___ d. Encourage creativity in the performance and application of course concepts.

17. ___ a. Change course materials or training methods based on update of expertise in the subject matter.
___ b. Begin a program by having learners introduce themselves to one another and communicate to trainer what their expectations are.
___ c. Adjust time schedules during the program in response to learners' interests and concerns.
___ d. Enhance credibility with learners by answering all questions quickly and accurately.

18. ___ a. Avoid potentially embarrassing questions and protect material by keeping content resources confidential.
___ b. Highlight key points in detail, speaking from carefully prepared notes.
___ c. Vary pace of the program to adjust to natural daily highs and lows in learners' energy levels.
___ d. Evaluate learners based on their abilities to perform specific objectives.

EXHIBIT 3.1. *Continued*

19. ___ a. Defend trainer's expertise and credibility when challenged by a learner on a content issue.

___ b. Emphasize establishing open, two-way communication.

___ c. Leave the structure of the program loose to respond to the specific needs of the group.

___ d. Aim the level of sophistication of course material at the "average" learner.

20. ___ a. Listen attentively and observe group discussion of content issues or problem applications.

___ b. Ensure that learners reach the right conclusions and accept the key points or concepts presented.

___ c. Explore reasons that learners ask questions, to bring out individual concerns and hidden agendas.

___ d. Project confidence and assurance by using effective gestures, posture, and vocal dynamics while instructing.

EXHIBIT 3.1. *Continued*   **INSTRUCTIONAL STYLES DIAGNOSIS INVENTORY SCORING SHEET**
(To be completed by trainer)

Step 1.

Instructions: Transfer the rankings from the ISDI to the Scoring Chart below. Note that the letter items in each set are not in alphabetical order.

Scoring Chart

	A	**B**	**C**	**D**
1	d	a	c	b
2	b	c	d	a
3	d	a	b	C
4	a	d	c	b
5	c	a	b	d
6	b	c	a	d
7	c	b	d	a
8	a	b	d	c
9	d	b	a	c
10	b	a	c	d
11	a	c	b	d
12	b	d	a	c
13	a	d	b	c
14	b	a	d	c
15	d	b	c	a
16	c	d	b	a
17	d	c	b	a
18	b	d	c	a
19	a	c	t	d
20	d	c	a	b
Total				

EXHIBIT 3.1. *Continued*

Step 2.

Determine the sum of the rankings in each column and record them at the bottom of that column.

Step 3.

Subtract the lower of the Column A and C totals from the higher.

Step 4.

Subtract the lower of the Column B and D totals from the higher.

Step 5.

Plot the result from Step 3 on the vertical scale of the graph that follows. If the "A" total is higher, plot the result below the midpoint "0." If the "C" total is higher, plot the result above this point.

Step 6.

Plot the result from Step 4 on the horizontal scale. If the "B" total is higher, plot the result to the right of the midpoint "0." If the "D" total is higher, plot the result to the left of this point.

Step 7.

Extend lines from the plotted points on each scale to the point where the two lines intersect.

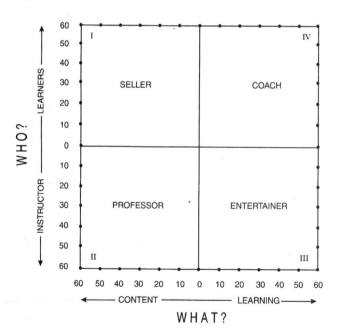

EXHIBIT 3.1. *Continued*

INSTRUCTIONAL STYLES DIAGNOSTIC INVENTORY
INTERPRETATION SHEET
(For the trainer)

COMPONENTS OF INSTRUCTIONAL STYLES

The styles that trainers use in developing and presenting learning experiences are based on their personal beliefs about what the purposes of instruction are and how they can best contribute to achieving those purposes.

The ISDI attempts to determine training style as the interactive product of two dimensions: what the trainer's attention is focused on and who is the focus of attention while the trainer is instructing. Each dimension is a function of two sets of concerns.

The what dimension (the horizontal scale) represents the tradeoff between:

1. Concern for content quality and thoroughness of presentation coverage (represented by the Column D total); and

2. Concern for the actual learning that takes place with learners who are working with the content (represented by the Column B total).

The who dimension (the vertical scale) represents the tradeoff between:

1. Concern for the trainer and how polished, impressive, or entertaining his or her delivery is (represented by the Column A total); and

2. Concern for the learners and how effectively or positively they are receiving, practicing, considering, discussing, or applying new skills (represented by the Column C total).

No model of this type is perfect. For instance, you may be able to think of trainers who are able to balance a high concern for content with a high concern for the learning that the content produces. However, for most instructors, it is realistic to expect that balancing the two involves influencing one at the expense of the other. The same may be said for the who dimension.

EXHIBIT 3.1. *Continued* **INTERPRETING YOUR SCORES**

The point on the graph at which the scores of these two dimensions intersect represents your overall training style.

To interpret your results, you must consider three things:

1. The comparative strengths of the four individual column totals,

2. The position of each of the two dimension scores, and

3. The direction and distance from the center of the point where the two dimension scores intersect.

For instance, were the four column totals high and low or were they close to one another? This indicates whether you tend to balance each aspect of training style equally or whether some aspects differ greatly to you in degree of importance. This directly affects the position of the dimension scores, which is the next consideration. If a dimension score is far toward one extreme or the other, this indicates a higher degree of tradeoff between the two sets of concerns involved. Dimension scores more near the middle represent a balanced degree of tradeoff, regardless of individual emphasis.

The intersection of the two dimension scores represents your overall training style, the product of your attempt to achieve balance among concerns for content, learning, delivery, and reception. The further this point is from the center of the graph, the more extreme your training style tends to be. The closer to the center this point is, the more "balanced" it tends to be.

DESCRIPTIONS OF STYLES

Following are short descriptions of the types of behaviors, attitudes, tendencies, and preferences that characterize each of the four styles.

I. "The Seller"

A person who has the "seller" instructional style is primarily concerned with the content and how positively it is received and understood. Learning is the participant's responsibility, and it may or may not happen as a result. Because getting the message across and creating a good attitude toward it are the primary goals, "seller" instructors tend to focus their attention on the learners and the learners' receptivity to the message.

They build a receptive atmosphere by creating a comfortable learning environment, encouraging learners, answering questions, varying the pace of the program, and so on. They tend to use lectures or prepared media presentation methods, interspersed with discussion to hold interest and attention. Note taking is encouraged to aid retention of material.

EXHIBIT 3.1. *Continued*

Homework, prework, and course-summary materials are used extensively to communicate or reinforce the content. Pass/fail or non-graded examinations are preferred to assess retention without turning the learners off.

The "seller" style is common in public schools and is probably more appropriate for building general educational backgrounds than for developing specific skills. It may also be appropriate for situations in which the selling of a technique, concept, or product is more important than the learners' becoming proficient in it. It is not as appropriate when learners are expected to perform better or differently as a result of the training.

II. "The Professor"

Instructors who have a high concern for both content and delivery probably see themselves primarily as presenters. The "professor" types tend to be highly concerned about such things as their image, their technique and smoothness of speaking, and creating a proper impression. They prefer to have the spotlight on themselves, because this focuses the learners' attention on them. The atmosphere in their sessions tends to be formal, and the separation between the presenter and the audience is emphasized.

"Professor" types are, at the same time, concerned with the adequacy of what they are presenting. Their presentations are usually well researched, often impressively footnoted and referenced, planned and organized in detail, and well rehearsed. Time is important because it reflects on their images as presenters (i.e., punctuality is impressive) and on their ability to cover all important content.

Their preferred teaching method is to lecture, as this allows them to focus attention on themselves, to control time, and to cover the content they believe is important. There is a tendency to overuse or inappropriately use media such as video, slides, or overheads because of their perceived ability to impress, entertain, and present large amounts of information in short time spans.

Typical situations where the "professor" style would be appropriate are: making a speech, delivering an after-dinner talk, communicating a report, and presenting or selling ideas to decision makers. This style usually is not as effective where actual skill development or behavioral change is expected from the learners. It may be appropriate for attitude change purposes; however, change produced by this method typically is short-lived unless constantly reinforced.

EXHIBIT 3.1. *Continued*

III. "The Entertainer"

Instructors who use the "entertainer" style focus on the results of training but also feel that people will learn best from instructors they like, respect, or admire. They have many of the same personal-image concerns as "professors." They are very concerned with their credibility and whether the learners have confidence in their expertise.

"Entertainers" are concerned about involvement in the learning process, but more with their own than with the learners'. Thus, methods such as watching a role model (the instructor) demonstrate proper technique are preferred over self-discovery or group learning activities. When more participatory methods are used, these instructors tend to exercise close control and make themselves an integral part of the learning process.

Because these instructors generally believe that learners need to be "inspired" if they are going to perform differently, sessions often are designed to be highly motivational or entertaining. This can be effective but has the potential limitation of making what is learned instructor dependent. When this occurs, learners can suffer drops in motivation when attempting to apply new skills on the job because the dynamic instructor is not there.

The fact that they are personally influencing learners is often more important to these instructors than the specific change that takes place or the input that caused it. Thus, specific content is not an important issue.

This style probably is most appropriate for personal growth seminars, sales meetings, and programs that are meant to "recharge learners' batteries."

In its worst case, the "entertainer" style could be likened to a medicine-show huckster who dazzles you and takes your money before you have a chance to judge the value of his product.

IV. "The Coach"

Instructors who are oriented both to learning and to the learners tend to have the spotlight reversed so that the learners' attention is focused on themselves most of the time. These trainers see their role more as facilitators of learning experiences than as presenters of information. They see value in course content only insofar as it enables learners to perform in new ways.

The focus of most coaching activities is on skill development, confidence building, and application, rather than on retention of information. Learners are evaluated, but mostly through observation of performance or behavioral change rather than through written tests. Grades usually are ignored, because most instruction is aimed at upgrading everyone's skills to a minimum or improved level rather than on determining who is most proficient.

EXHIBIT 3.1. *Continued*

There is less concern for polished delivery because "coach" instructors spend much less time "delivering." Also, because of the informal atmosphere created, there is less pressure on the instructor to perform, motivate, or entertain. Use of a high ratio of self-discovery and group learning activities allows the learners to motivate and entertain themselves. The responsibility to perform is, in effect, shifted from the instructor to them.

Separation between the instructor and the learners is deemphasized. The prevailing philosophy typically is that the best instructor is the one who sets high expectations, guides and coaches the learners, and then gets out of the way so they can perform.

The instructor has a message, but the message is determined more by specific learner needs and less by what the instructor thinks might be good for the learners. Rather than forcing learners to understand and accept new ideas, "coaches" use questions, discussions, self-study, group work, and other involving techniques to lead learners to conclusions, but they allow the learners to make the commitments on their own.

The "coach" style tends to be most effective in bona fide training situations where skill building and behavioral change are the primary concerns. Potential problems with this style are tendencies to ignore time constraints, skip over important content issues, lose control of the class, turn off learners who are used to more traditional instructional styles, or be overly influenced by learners' perceptions of their own needs.

EXHIBIT 3.1. *Continued*   **A QUICK REFERENCE SHEET**

The following figure provides an overview of the instructional styles measured by the Instructional Styles Diagnostic Instrument.

ISDI Quick Reference Guide

SELLER	COACH
Sellers are: Task oriented	Coaches are: Learner oriented
They see themselves as: Taskmasters/persuaders	They see themselves as: Facilitators/guides
Sellers' main concern is: Product/content	Coaches' main concern is: Results/performance
They strive to be: Driving, aggressive, enthusiastic, convincing	They strive to be: Participative, accepting, empathic, supportive
Programs are structured to be: Informal but inflexible	Programs are structured to be: Informal and flexible
Leading to sessions that are: Informative, productive, efficient, complete, persuasive	Leading to sessions that are: Involving, encouraging, constructive, developmental
Learners are evaluated by: Objective testing	Learners are evaluated by: Comparing behaviors or performance objectives
PROFESSOR	**ENTERTAINER**
Professors are: Instructor oriented	Entertainers are: Relations oriented
They see themselves as: Presenters/experts	They see themselves as: Role models/stars
Professors' main concern is: Process/delivery	Entertainers' main concern is: Reactions/feelings
They strive to be: Impressive, polished, professional, aloof	They strive to be: Dynamic, animated, charismatic, outgoing, inspirational
Programs are structured to be: Formal and inflexible	Programs are structured to be: Formal but flexible
Leading to sessions that are: Scheduled, controlled, organized, disciplined	Leading to sessions that are: Motivated, lively, fun, entertaining
Learners are evaluated by: Subjective testing and instructor judgment	Learners are evaluated by: Assessment of their feelings and opinions

WHO — LEARNERS / INSTRUCTOR

◄— CONTENT —————— LEARNING —►
WHAT?

Increasing Effectiveness

As mentioned in the description of styles in the interpretation section of the *Instructional Styles Diagnosis Inventory,* the "coach" is probably the most appropriate style for a true training situation. This style and its underlying philosophy are reflected throughout this book. The coaching style supports and reinforces the cooperative-learning approach to training adults.

Keep in mind, however, that the coaching style is not going to be appropriate for every learner. The challenge is to increase style flexibility and learn to assess what style or approach is the most appropriate with a particular situation, group, or individual learner. Flexibility is the key to success, that is, changing and adapting throughout the training program as you are faced with new challenges from the participants. Trainers have trouble when they either cannot or will not adapt to the styles and needs of the participants.

LEARNER-CENTERED VERSUS INFORMATION-CENTERED

To better understand the difference between learner-centered and information-centered learning, study Figure 3.1. Notice that with learner-centered training, the primary focus is on what the learner or participant is able to take away from the learning experience. The learner is actively involved in the process and, therefore, is much more likely to retain the information and be able to apply it on the job.

Advantages and Disadvantages

Both learner-centered training and information-centered training have advantages and disadvantages, as seen in Figure 3.2. Although research supports learner-centered instruction over information-centered, the reality of life is that sometimes "the powers that be" apply pressure on trainers to put massive numbers of people through so-called "training" in a short period of time. Although we know that this "cattle-car" approach to training is not effective, it is often difficult to convince others. Regardless of whether you are an internal or an external practitioner, if your client—the decision maker—insists on what amounts to the simple dissemination of information, you may want to suggest an alternative approach. Alternatives may include sending required reading material to employees, creating an audiotape or videotape of a presentation, or even communicating via the organization's intranet system. Be sure to stress that these other approaches should not be mistaken for training. They are one-way communication methods designed to present information.

FIGURE 3.1. Learner-Centered versus Information-Centered Training

	Learner-Centered	*Information-Centered*
Stated Objective	To improve performance of participants	To cover the material; present content
Underlying Objectives	Meet participants' need to know and do	To establish trainer as expert
Role of Trainer	Facilitator; coach	Imparter of information; lecturer
Methods	Trainer asks questions; does no more than 50% of the talking	Trainer lectures, explains, demonstrates; does most of the talking while participants listen and watch
Participant's Role	Active participant in learning process; learns by doing	Passive learner; absorbs information
How Feedback Is Obtained	Opportunities to apply skills through role plays, case studies, simulations, and other structured experiences	Asking participants if they have any questions; asking participants questions about what trainer has said
Purpose of Feedback	To see if participants can apply what they learned; to see if they need more practice or remedial instruction	To see if participants understand the information; to test their retention

FIGURE 3.2. Learner-Centered Training and Information-Centered Training: Advantages and Disadvantages

	Learner-Centered	*Information-Centered*
Advantages	Participants directly involved in learning; opportunities to apply learning	Efficient—more information presented in short period of time
	Participants receive immediate feedback through application opportunities	Effective in presenting "nice to know" rather than "need to know" information
	Greater satisfaction with learning experience	Cost effective—one trainer can present to many people at once
	Increased understanding and retention	
	Addresses different learning styles	
	Two-way communication	
Disadvantages	Takes longer because participants have opportunities to practice	Information overload often results in poor retention
	Less content covered in a given time period	Participants' questions often are not addressed
	Can be expensive because of smaller class size	Less satisfaction with learning experience
		Limited effectiveness in appealing to differences in learning styles
		Participants have no opportunity to apply learning during the training session and receive feedback
		One-way communication

Recognizing Learner-Centered Behavior

To test your understanding of learner-centered versus information-centered behavior, complete the activity in Exhibit 3.2. You could also use this checklist as a reminder of what you need to do to become more learner-centered in your training sessions. Answers are provided in Appendix A.

KEY ELEMENTS OF A TRAINER'S STYLE

As you work through this text, you will be challenged to examine and perhaps even to modify your own beliefs and practices. Should you decide to make some changes in your current thinking or behaviors, realize that change is not easy. In fact, it can be downright painful. When it seems that changing the way you train (or had planned to train) is just too much work, ask yourself the following questions: "Am I as effective a trainer as I would like to be?" and "Am I obtaining the results I want?" If the answers to these questions are "no," then be open to learning and trying out new ways of structuring and conducting your training sessions. Use the following list of behaviors as a reminder for creating participant-centered training:

- Organize the program and behave in such a way that participants feel that they have "ownership" of the program.
- Create many opportunities for participants to discover things for themselves.
- Establish both participant and trainer expectations at the very beginning of the program.
- Create a supportive learning environment in which people feel free to take risks, to ask questions, and to try out new ideas and ways of doing things.
- Be sensitive to the communication process, including your own body language as well as that of your participants.
- Maintain a high energy level throughout the session. It becomes contagious.
- Accept ideas you may not agree with, and accept the fact that some people will not agree with you.
- Show respect to all participants, no matter how difficult they may be.
- Do not be afraid to admit what you do not know; be willing to find out the information and pass it on to the participants later.
- Use positive reinforcement throughout the session.

EXHIBIT 3.2 Learner-Centered or Information-Centered Behavior

Instructions: For each of the following items, indicate whether it is descriptive of learner-centered (LC) or information-centered (IC) behavior.

1. ____ The job of a trainer should be to present the material in a clear, logical, well-organized manner.

2. ____ At the beginning of a training session, the trainer clearly identifies the session or course objectives.

3. ____ The trainer encourages participants to ask questions when they need clarification.

4. ____ Visual aids are used minimally.

5. ____ The trainer uses tests to find out how well the participants retained the material.

6. ____ The trainer begins a session by reviewing ground rules dealing with breaks.

7. ____ The most important factor to consider when evaluating packaged training programs is the amount of content.

8. ____ The best trainer is one who involves the participants.

9. ____ The room is arranged classroom style with participants seated in rows, all facing the trainer.

10. ____ Good trainers are experts in their subject matter.

11. ____ Experience and knowledge of subject are more important than the ability to involve the participants in the learning experience.

12. ____ The trainer asks participants what they want to know and learn.

13. ____ The trainer builds in many opportunities to try out new skills and ideas.

14. ____ The trainer establishes himself or herself as the expert or authority on the subject.

15. ____ The trainer's role is to facilitate the learning process.

16. ____ The trainer frequently puts participants into small groups to discuss questions or solve problems.

17. ____ The trainer chooses a variety of learning methods or approaches.

18. ____ The primary role of the participant is to receive information from the trainer or subject-matter expert.

- Look at every training experience as an opportunity to learn from your participants.
- Make the learning experience enjoyable.
- Seek feedback from the group about your own behavior so that you can further grow and develop as a trainer.

You will learn specific strategies throughout the book that reflect participant-centered trainer behavior and will help you create a powerful learning experience for all.

◆ ◆ ◆

Module Four

Understanding Today's Learner

LEARNING OUTCOMES

In this module, you will learn

- To identify the diversity issues that impact the design, development, and delivery of training
- To use tools and techniques to create a risk-free and bias-free learning environment

THE CHANGING TRAINING ENVIRONMENT

Organizational training has changed dramatically in the last decade and will continue to change well into the next century. A more diverse work force has not only changed the way companies do business but also the way they train their workers. In addition to different learning styles, differences such as age, gender, race, ethnicity, life styles, religion, language, disabilities, and literacy impact how trainers design, develop, and deliver training. The challenge of meeting the individual needs of participants often seems overwhelming. Armed with an understanding of today's learners and equipped with a tool kit of tips and techniques, you as a change agent and influencer of behavior will be able to create an environment that both respects and celebrates differences.

SELF-AWARENESS

To be effective in meeting the needs of a diverse audience, first examine your own attitudes, beliefs, and behaviors toward those who are different from you. Your own unintentional biases and inadvertent insensitivity may undermine your attempts to create an environment that values the individual and promotes learning. To increase your self-awareness of the ways in which your behavior and beliefs are transferred to the workshop, complete the "Diversity Awareness Inventory" in Exhibit 4.1.

There is, of course, no score for this assessment. Its purpose is to help you identify areas in which you might need to acquire information or make a concerted effort to modify your behavior.

EXHIBIT 4.1. Diversity Awareness Inventory

Instructions: This inventory is designed to increase your awareness of the ways in which you judge, stereotype, and sometimes discriminate. Please respond to each of the following statements by placing a check mark in the appropriate column.

	No	Yes	Some-times
1. I recognize that I have prejudices and biases.	___	___	___
2. I make efforts to learn to know people from cultures and races other than my own.	___	___	___
3. I accept that other people may not share my values, views, or life style.	___	___	___
4. I try to learn about other cultures by reading and asking questions.	___	___	___
5. I try not to judge others by my own behavior or standards.	___	___	___
6. I help people from other cultures learn about mine.	___	___	___
7. I respect other cultures' traditions and practices.	___	___	___
8. I make certain to include examples, case studies, and other types of activities that reflect the diversity in my training group.	___	___	___
9. I create an environment in which all participants feel free to express and be themselves.	___	___	___
10. I make a special effort to become familiar with the ways that other cultures communicate verbally and nonverbally.	___	___	___

DIVERSITY ISSUES

The most important thing to remember is that you are training individuals who just happen to be in a group setting. Before dealing with specific design and delivery considerations, let's look at some specific diversity issues. Although many diversity categories may be represented in the workshop, let's focus on those that have the greatest impact on workshop climate.

Age Differences

The so-called "generation gap" seems to be widening more and more throughout the world, particularly in corporate America. At one end of the workplace continuum are the young professionals in their early twenties; at the other end are the older employees, for whom the idea of an early, comfortable retirement is a fast-fading concept. The result is a much greater age span in the workplace than ever before. The U.S. work force is aging; by the year 2005, those over age fifty-five will make up 15 percent of the work force. The median age of workers will be forty-five by 2000.

Meeting the Training Needs of Older Participants As noted in Module Two, the ability to learn does not diminish with age. There are those, however, who believe that anyone over forty cannot learn new skills. Forty, the somewhat arbitrary number that separates "younger" worker from "older" worker, seems to stem from the Age Discrimination in Employment Act of 1967, designed to protect workers over forty from unfair employment policies and practices. Trainers make statements such as, "Older workers don't catch on as quickly" or "Older people can't adapt to change." These beliefs are bound to be reflected in the trainer's behavior toward older participants. According to Harvey Sterns, director of the Institute for Lifespan Development and Gerontology (Sterns & Doverspike, 1988), many people over forty may indeed take longer to learn new skills, primarily because they have to first unlearn the way they are currently doing things. Younger employees who have grown up with computers and video games will, of course, find it easier to learn new computer systems and software programs than will their older colleagues who learned to use typewriters and carbon paper.

One of the biggest barriers to older workers learning new skills is their lack of confidence or fear of failure, created, in part, by society's myths and stereotypes about aging. So the trainer's first challenge is to build older participants' confidence by encouraging them. Hands-on learning is even more critical for those over forty, as well as using materials and methods that are directly job-focused and relevant to the participants' work situations. Because some older adults experience a decline in vision or hearing, the trainer must pay attention to the room arrangement, lighting, and the use of larger print on visual aids and in participant workbooks.

Those thirty-five and older are interested in receiving training that is relevant, immediately applicable, and in an easy-to-absorb format. Participants over thirty-five are in a hurry to learn. They realize that they must keep up and, in some cases, catch up in order to survive in today's fast-paced, high-pressure, and rapidly changing work environment.

Connecting with Younger Participants Younger workers, the so-called "Generation X" born during the years from 1965 to 1979, present a different challenge. Many erroneous assumptions are made about them as well. Trainers as well as managers may think that these younger workers have a short attention span, are disrespectful, apathetic, lazy, and think they know it all. The truth is that they are enthusiastic, confident, and achievement-oriented. They can process large amounts of data at a time; however, they want information presented in abbreviated forms such as sound bites and checklists. These characteristics create different challenges as well as opportunities for trainers.

During the training event, these participants need many opportunities to apply their knowledge and solve problems through group discussion, simulations, case studies, and so forth. They like to be challenged but also want to receive immediate and meaningful feedback. They are easily bored and, therefore, programs must be designed that offer a variety of learning experiences. The entertainment factor cannot be overlooked. Remember: This is the MTV generation. They expect high-quality materials, including participant workbooks, videos, and other visual aids.

Because they like to challenge as well as be challenged, they will question and demand proof of what is being said. They will not accept your word at face value just because you are the trainer. Be prepared with facts and figures to support your statements and explain why you are teaching a particular skill or piece of information, focusing particularly on outcomes and results. They do not like to be told what to do, so provide opportunities for them to discover things on their own through structured experiences and self-assessment instruments.

SAMPLE ATTITUDES OF YOUNGER WORKERS

I conducted a problem-solving and decision-making session for new associates in a Wall Street investment firm. These recent college graduates were the "cream of the crop"—intelligent, well-educated, energetic, enthusiastic, and clearly "fast-trackers." They came to the session with the confidence and bravado that are typical of the uninitiated. They expressed early that they thought the session was a waste of time because they knew how to make decisions and solve problems. Rather than argue with them, I put them into small groups and gave them a rather complicated business simulation in which they had to analyze six problem situations and come up with solutions. They were given fifteen minutes to solve each problem and then were given the recommended solution so they could score their teams before moving on to the next situation.

Without exception, all five groups quickly arrived at the solution to the first problem and waited impatiently for the correct answer. Much to their surprise, they were all wrong. Thinking this was just a fluke, they quickly solved the next problem and were wrong on that one, too. Getting the message that this was not as easy and simplistic as they first thought, they began to buckle down and took the time to look beneath the surface and beyond the obvious. When they finished the last four problems, they were not only exhausted but humbled because they realized and readily admitted that they had not known as much about solving problems as they had thought they did.

Because many have grown up as latch-key kids, today's younger participants have learned to be self-reliant and independent problem solvers. To function in the current work environment, they must be involved in learning experiences that will help them develop the interpersonal and team skills they lack.

It is even more critical that these younger employees participate in planning the training program and that self-study and projects outside the structured environment be included.

Today's audiences, regardless of age, are conditioned by television, and consequently, they expect to take frequent "commercial breaks" of sorts. The training design must reflect the participants' need to stand up and move around or at least experience a change in venue or delivery methods.

Gender Differences

Gender issues continue to exist in corporations and find their way into corporate training. As a role model, you must demonstrate appropriate behavior at all times. Make sure task assignments are evenly distributed to both genders, preventing participants from falling into traditional roles such as a woman recording and a man leading the discussion. The trainer must also avoid using sexist remarks or examples and activities that appeal more to one gender.

Help bridge the gender gap by providing opportunities to heighten awareness of the different perspectives each gender brings to the same situation. Promote this exchange of perspectives through small-group activities, making sure all groups include both men and women. During general discussions, solicit ideas and reactions from both men and women.

Cultural Differences

Today's corporate training room is a patchwork quilt of many cultures that can enrich the learning experience. Learn how to draw on the experience and background of these participants to add value to training, regardless of the topic. You have a responsibility to understand and meet the learning needs of those whose experiences and frames of reference may be quite different from yours. Create opportunities for participants from different backgrounds to learn about one another by working together in structured experiences.

Accommodating Differences

Cultural differences include ethnicity, race, gender, age, and affiliations. When selecting both methods and materials, make sure to choose videos, case studies, and other activities that are inclusive and reflect diverse audiences.

Materials Eliminate gender-specific language, such as chairman, mailman, fireman, or salesman. Instead, use chairperson, postal carrier, fire fighter, or salesperson. Role plays and case studies should reflect various cultures in the choice of names and situations. If you are writing your own, be careful not to create profiles or situations that illustrate and thus perpetuate stereotypes. For example, in a role play or case study illustrating an interaction between a manager and an employee, make sure that the manager is not always identified as a white male and the employee as a female or a minority person.

For case studies, select names that clearly reflect the diversity in your organization such as Kwan Lee, Jose, Rosa, Tamera, Antonio, or Amalia. For role-play assignments, use gender-neutral names like Robin, Pat, Chris, or Kim. Or indicate that the role can be either gender by expressing both: Robert or Roberta, Sam or Samantha, Michael or Michele.

If you purchase a packaged program or use published materials authored by someone else, make sure they meet these same criteria or alter them as needed. Use similar care in choosing videos that reflect diversity. The same holds true for graphics you add to participant workbooks or those included in materials purchased from a training vendor.

Trainer Behavior Think about the different ways in which people from various cultures communicate, both verbally and nonverbally, so that you can prevent communication miscues. For example, you may interpret head nodding to mean that the participant is agreeing with what you are saying. In some cultures, however, nodding one's head is only an indication that the person is listening and is also encouraging the speaker to continue. In U.S. culture, people often make negative judgments about those who do not engage in direct eye contact. Once again, other cultures view direct eye contact as challenging or disrespectful. It is important that you not misinterpret a participant's behavior that may be culturally based.

Learning about your participants also includes learning how to pronounce their names and addressing them correctly during the workshop.

SAMPLE OF DIVERSE EXPECTATIONS

I learned the importance of using people's names the hard way in a session on influencing skills for a group of new associates in a bank. The members of the group were in their early twenties with an equal distribution of women and men. The group, however, was quite diverse in terms of cultural backgrounds, with a mix of those from North America, Asia, the Middle East, and the Indian subcontinent. One young man from Afghanistan was particularly interesting and very participative. He spoke with me at length during breaks and at lunch, and seemed to have developed rapport with me. I was, therefore, quite surprised to read on his evaluation of the session that he was offended because I had not made any attempt during the day to say his name. He was not the only person who was not addressed specifically by name. In his culture, however, addressing a person by name is very important, and he felt that I had demonstrated disrespect by not doing so.

To avoid similar incidents, make an effort to learn about those from other cultures by talking with them and asking them questions about their customs. Ask the correct pronunciation of their names and then practice saying them. Read articles and books about intercultural communication so that you are somewhat familiar with the cultures that are most frequently represented in your training sessions.

Activities Keep in mind that in many cultures, the approach to learning is very traditional. The trainer is regarded as an authority figure. Participants are expected to assume a passive role, with the trainer delivering content in a very structured and rigid manner. As a result, some people may be uncomfortable with the participative and interactive approach to learning. These participants may need a little more nudging and encouragement to help increase their comfort level with the learning process. Cooperative-learning techniques such as asking people to discuss a question or problem in pairs or small groups are effective ways of involving those who are not accustomed to interactive learning.

PARTICIPANTS WITH DISABILITIES

Today's training audiences represent a variety of special needs and considerations. Some participants will have one or more disabilities. As with other differences, be sensitive to their situations, accommodate their special needs, but at the same time, be sensitive to their need to be treated just like everyone else.

Accommodating Disabilities

It is incumbent upon you to learn how to adapt training methods and materials to accommodate the needs of participants with physical, mental, and even medical impairments. Find out in advance about those who may have special needs and accommodate those needs in the initial design.

For example, if a hearing-impaired person will be attending the session, find out whether an interpreter will be accompanying the individual or, if not, to what degree the participant can read lips. If lip reading is required, make sure the participant is positioned in such a way that he or she is able to see your face. You, of course, must make sure to turn toward that individual when speaking. When other participants respond to a question or make a comment, remind them to do the same, if possible.

Be sensitive to those who may have learning disabilities, literacy problems, or for whom English is a second language. Choose or create materials written at an appropriate reading level. This is where a pre-session questionnaire or other needs-assessment methods can be especially helpful. Know as much as you can about the individuals who will be attending your session! Do not make assumptions about people just because they hold particular jobs or are at certain levels within the organization.

EXAMPLES OF ACCOMMODATING DISABILITIES

I was asked to conduct a multi-session business-writing program for bank managers and assistant managers. About halfway through the program, just at the time when assignments became more complex, one of the participants (a branch manager) came to me after the session and explained that she was having a very difficult time writing the assigned letters and memos. She had dyslexia, and not only did no one in the bank know about her learning disability, but she did not want them to know. I worked with her one-on-one either before or after the workshop.

In another situation, I was conducting a four-session supervisory-training program for twelve first-line supervisors in a manufacturing environment. At the first session, eleven of the twelve came to the training session. The next evening, the man who had missed the first day called me at home. He apologized for missing the session, and he wanted to explain why. He said that he had heard from the others that the session was really good and he wanted to come but was afraid to because he would have to read "stuff" and discuss it. He explained that he was concerned because he could not read, and he did not want others to know. I assured him that he would be able to participate and that his colleagues would never know. To accommodate his special need, I either read or paraphrased the assignment before they broke into small groups.

Activities It is also a good idea to provide written materials and to write instructions for activities and exercises on a flip chart or transparency. Be sure to think through the logistics of activities, keeping in mind participants with special needs. Be aware that you cannot anticipate everything. No matter how well you plan, sometimes you will be caught off guard.

EXAMPLE OF FLEXIBILITY

I was contracted by the Pennsylvania Industries for the Blind and Handicapped to present a customer-service program to their employees who staffed the photo license centers throughout Pennsylvania. Many of the participants had some visual impairment and several were in wheelchairs.

Because I used many small-group activities throughout the day, requiring people to change groups, I arranged the room so that those in wheelchairs would be able to move about as easily as possible. I also accommodated the needs of those who were visually impaired by reading materials as appropriate. Despite all the planning and preparation, there was still a surprise. One of the participants was deaf and her interpreter did not show up. Although the participant was able to read lips, I had to make a last-minute adjustment in an activity that was designed to illustrate poor listening skills.

Adapting Materials Many special needs are obvious, but there are many others that are difficult to detect unless someone brings them to our attention. One good technique to move people quickly into small groups is called a "grouping card," which will be explained in more detail in Module Eleven. Each person receives a card that includes a colored dot. To form a specific small-group arrangement, ask participants to group themselves according to the color of their dots. This works well unless someone is color-blind. An alternative is to use various shapes and symbols instead.

As a trainer, you have a responsibility to create a learning environment in which all participants feel free to express themselves and be themselves.

Begin to create this environment when you design a program, taking into consideration all types of differences, including learning-style differences. Not only respect the individual differences of those in your sessions, but make sure to incorporate into the design a variety of methods and materials that will accommodate those differences.

◆ ◆ ◆

Module Five

Writing Instructional Objectives

LEARNING OUTCOMES

In this module, you will learn

- To determine the desired performance-based outcomes based on the needs analysis
- To write properly constructed learning objectives
- To use outcomes or objectives as the basis for program design and development

---

WHAT ARE LEARNING OBJECTIVES?

After the needs assessment has been completed and the data gathered, analyzed, and reported to the appropriate people, the next step is to design the training program. The first step in the design process is to write learning objectives.

Learning objectives or outcomes state what the learner will be able to do at the end of the training program or at the end of a phase of training. They describe the planned outcome of the training rather than the training process—results rather than procedures.

Why Set Objectives?

Objectives serve as a type of contract. If participants know the program or session objectives from the beginning, they will know what they are expected to learn. Objectives give participants a sense of direction. They know what to expect from you and what you expect from them.

Objectives serve as the basis for the design and development of the program, that is, the instructional plan. They help the trainer focus clearly on the desired outcomes and determine what the participants need to know and do in order to meet those objectives. The concept of designing a training program is analogous to planning a trip: the objectives are the destination and the instructional plan is the itinerary. First decide where you want to go (objectives) and then decide how you are going to get there—how long the trip will take and what means of transportation you will use (methods and materials).

Objectives should be written from the participant's point of view, not the trainer's. The emphasis should not be on what you want to cover but on what you want the participant to value, understand, or do with the subject, information, or skills after the training program is over.

Objectives are used to measure success. Because they describe what the participant will be able to do at the end of the training, the objectives automatically become the standard against which success is measured.

Finally, objectives are a sales tool. Develop the program objectives based on the needs assessment conducted earlier. Then use these objectives to tell the participants' managers exactly what your training will do for their employees. These managers will have a much better understanding of what the training will and will not do.

Types of Objectives

Objectives fall into three categories of skill development: *attitude* (affective), *skill* (behavioral), and *knowledge* (cognitive).

Attitude Development Objectives that address attitude development deal with attitudes, values, or feelings. These objectives are appropriate when you want to change people's attitudes or increase their awareness of or sensitivity to certain issues or ideas.

Skill Development Objectives for skill development deal with behavior. These are much easier to identify and to determine if they have been met. They focus on being able to perform a task or procedure.

Knowledge Development Knowledge-development objectives have to do with content or cognitive learning. They relate to the ability to demonstrate acquired knowledge, to comprehend information, and to analyze concepts.

Essential Characteristics of Objectives

For objectives to be useful, they must meet certain criteria. They must be:

- *Objective and Measurable.* Objectives should describe exactly what the participant will be able to do at the end of the training session, that is, specify the kind of behavior (if possible) that will be accepted as evidence that the participant has achieved the objective.
- *Results-Oriented, Clearly Worded, and Specific.*
- *Focused Only on Important Aspects of the Job.*
- *Measurable with Both Qualitative and Quantitative Criteria.*
- *Action-Oriented Statements.* They must outline specific activities and how performance will be measured.
- *Written in Terms of Performance.* The trainer can then select the most appropriate methods and activities.
- *Specific About What the Participants Will Be Able to Do.* They must be specific about results, rather than describing the trainer or the experience of the session.
- *Descriptive of the Participants' Behavior or Performance.* Objectives should not describe what participants must know or understand, but what participants must do to demonstrate their understanding, knowledge, or skill.
- *Descriptive of Desired Competence at the End of the Training.*
- *Specific About the Conditions Under Which the Participants Will Be Performing.*
- *Indicative of the Minimum Level of Performance Acceptable.*

Components of an Objective

Writing objectives is not an easy task. The first challenge is to think of objectives from the participants' viewpoint, and the second challenge is to write them as performance outcomes. The easiest way to write an objective is to start by examining its three components: *performance*, *condition*, and *criteria*.

Performance Ideally, the objective should describe behavior that can be observed, that is, what the participant will be able to do as a result of the training. This is not always possible, particularly when dealing with attitude or affective objectives. When the objective is not observable, specify the consequences of the learned behavior that can be accepted as evidence of achievement. For example, for a diversity-training program, an objective might be to "increase the participant's awareness of and sensitivity to workplace diversity issues."

The objective contains specific action verbs that are not subject to various interpretations. Words such as *understand, know,* and *learn,* for example, are not acceptable. You cannot observe those behaviors. Figure 5.1 offers a few action verbs for each of the desired learning outcomes. For example, a performance component for a sales-training objective might be to "suggest other bank services to the customer."

FIGURE 5.1. Reference Chart for Objectives

Learning Type	Related Action Verbs	
Attitude Development	adjust	decide
	analyze	evaluate
	assess	pick
	choose	select
	criticize	
Skill Development	assemble	prepare
	compute	process
	construct	prove
	copy	record
	count	repair
	demonstrate	solve
	design	speak
	develop	transcribe
	draw	type
	measure	write
	operate	
Knowledge Development	cite	identify
	compare	list
	contrast	name
	define	quote
	describe	recite
	detect	recognize
	differentiate	relate
	distinguish	repeat
	enumerate	reproduce
	explain	

Condition The objective explains the circumstances under which the participant will be performing the activity. It also describes the equipment, supplies, and job aids that may or may not be used on the job. Furthermore, the objective describes the work setting and any information used to direct the action. For example, a statement such as "Using open-ended questions to identify customer needs, the participant will . . ." identifies the materials the participant will use to help him or her perform an action.

Criteria Finally, the objective specifies the level or degree of proficiency that is necessary to perform the task or job successfully. It indicates the quality of the performance required to achieve objectives. Thus, information in the criteria is used to evaluate performance. The objective may involve speed, accuracy with a margin of error, maximum number of mistakes permitted, productivity level, or degree of excellence. Keep in mind that not all standards can be quantified. Following the sales example, a criterion might be to identify how many or which services the participant would tell the customer about. Putting it all together, the objective reads: "Using open-ended questions to identify the customer's needs (*condition*), the participant will suggest (*performance*) at least two additional products or services to every customer (*criterion*)."

To gain a better understanding of the format and components of an objective, take a look at the following examples:

- "Using brochures and desk-top charts (condition), customer-service representatives will answer (performance) all customer questions about standard products and services (criteria)."
- "Employees will answer the telephone (performance) within three rings (criterion) using the standard identification message and greeting (condition)."
- "Following prescribed bank procedures (condition), employees will balance the teller windows (performance) each day within twenty minutes (criterion)."
- "Using PowerPoint® software (condition), employees will create (performance) a thirty-minute presentation that includes animation and sound (criteria)."
- "Managers will write (performance) a two-page, error-free request proposal (criteria) following the proposal format introduced in the business-writing workshop (condition)."

WRITING LEARNING OBJECTIVES

To help you gain a better understanding of how to write learning objectives, complete the activity in Exhibit 5.1.

EXHIBIT 5.1. Editing Learning Objectives

Instructions: Examine each of the following objectives from a leadership program and decide if it is a well-stated learning objective. If not, change it so that it is acceptable, noting what component needs to be added.

- Develop an understanding of the leader's role.

- Know the difference between authority of rank and authority of respect.

- Understand the theories of motivation.

- Know the characteristics of a leader.

- Know the role of the manager in a team environment.

- Appreciate the advantages and disadvantages involved in group decision making.

- Identify ways to motivate employees.

Using an Objective Worksheet

To better understand and master the objective-writing process, take a look at the "Sample Workshop Objectives Worksheet" in Figure 5.2, which identifies the component parts of a well-written objective.

FIGURE 5.2. Sample Workshop Objectives Worksheet

Subject: Leadership Characteristics	
Condition • What participants will be given • Tools, supplies, equipment • Use of notes, simulated situation	*Results from several recent studies*
Behavior/Action • What participants will be doing • Emphasis on verb • What can be observed	*Identify*
Criteria • What standards apply • Time limits • Degree of accuracy • Level of performance	*Six characteristics of effective leaders in a team environment*

On the left are the components of a well-written objective along with a breif explanation of what information is included in each component. To the right of each component is an example of the specific piece(s) of information that would satisfy that component. In this example, the subject is "leadership characterisics." The objective (taken from the previous activity) "Know the characteristics of a leader" is not specific enough. In fact, this objective does not even come close to meeting the criteria listed earlier.

In this particular example, the trainer will be giving the participants "results from several recent studies" (condition). Having given that information, the trainer then expects the participants to be able to "identify" (behavior) "six characteristics of effective leaders in a team environment" (criteria). As you can see, the worksheet can help you identify the components more easily. You can then put those components together to create a useful and meaningul leaning objective: "Using the results of several recent studies on leadership, participants will identify the six characteristics of effective leaders in a team environment."

Writing Your Own Objectives

Choose a particular topic from your own situation and write three learning objectives that include all three components. Use the "Workshop Objectives Worksheet" in Figure 5.3.

FIGURE 5.3. Workshop Objectives Worksheet

Subject:

Instructions: In the space to the right of each item, write the specific pieces(s) of information that will be used to satisfy that component.

Condition

- What participant will be given

- Tools, supplies, equipment

- Use of notes, simulated situation

Behavior/Action

- What participants will be doing

- Emphasis on verb

- What can be observed

Criteria

- What standards apply

- Time limits

- Degree of accuracy

- Level of performance

At first, the practice of writing objectives may seem difficult, tedious, and time-consuming. With practice, though, it will become easy. After you have determined learning outcomes and written objectives, you are ready to design your training program.

✦ ✦ ✦

Module Six

Writing an Instructional Plan

LEARNING OUTCOMES

In this module you will learn

- To develop a clear and complete design matrix
- To write an instructional plan
- To select appropriate methods of instruction
- To determine how to sequence content and activities
- To develop and select appropriate participant and trainer materials

---

DESIGN PHILOSOPHY

The training approach described in this book can be summarized in one word: *active*. The underlying philosophy, as described in Module Two, is that adult participants are actively involved throughout the training session. The design and development strategies, therefore, reflect an active, experiential approach to training, allowing participants to discover ideas, principles, and concepts through a series of well-planned and well-executed structured experiences. Because the adult, in particular, learns by doing, not by being told, the design and development process includes very few didactic elements.

TIME NEEDED TO DEVELOP A TRAINING PROGRAM

The most frequently asked question in train-the-trainer sessions is "How long does it take to design and develop a training program?" The answer: "It depends." As frustrating as that might be to those who need to know how much time they must devote to this effort, there are just too many variables to give an accurate answer. A rule of thumb is ten to twenty hours of development for every hour of delivery.

However, this figure can change dramatically. In the September 1996 issue of *Training & Development,* published by the American Society for Training and Development, author Karen White tells the reader that a good estimate is "forty to one hundred hours of development for each hour of an instructor-led course." The May 1997 issue of *Training* magazine cites a study by the U.S. Office of Personnel Management, which offers the following estimates for development hours per classroom hour for an instructor-led course (Zemke & Armstrong, 1997).

Formal technical course   5–15 hours

Self-contained, ready for handoff to other instructors   50–100 hours

Conventional management development   20–30 hours

As you can see, all estimates give a wide range. Contributing variables include the designer's skill and experience, the complexity of the content, and whether one develops activities or uses those already developed. Will you use an "off-the-shelf" case study or will you write your own? Do you have the skills to write a case study? If you choose to use one that is already written, will you use it as written or will you modify it for a specific situation? Also, can you readily find an appropriate case study, or will you have to spend time looking through various resources to find one that serves your purposes? These are all critical decisions that involve varying amounts of time to produce the training session.

Designing a training program is much like planning a trip. In both cases, you must ask yourself the following questions:

	Trip	**Training Session**
Who	"Who is going?"	"Who should participate?"
When	"When are we going?"	"When will I conduct the training?"
Where	"Where are we going?"	"Where am I taking the participants (in terms of outcomes)?"

Why	"Why have we chosen this destination?"	"Why am I conducting this training?"
What	"What do we want to see and do?"	"What do I want the participants to know or be able to do?"
How	"How will we get there?"	"How will I communicate the information or develop the participants' skills?"

The reality of life is that others will often dictate how much time is available to develop the training program. Because situations change so rapidly and unexpectedly, you may not have the luxury of developing a training program the way you would like. For a new-product launch, for example, your client or decision maker may require you to put together a training session literally overnight.

Also, like it or not, your client may also dictate how long the session can be. Based on your needs assessment and your training experience, you may know that a customer-service training program should be at least two days. This would give you enough time to present the content and give participants many opportunities to assimilate the information through experiential activities and to fine-tune their skills through a variety of skill-building activities. More often than not, however, you will be told that the training must be limited to one day. This is why it is extremely important to identify your objectives quite clearly. Be realistic about what you can and cannot accomplish within the prescribed time frame.

The time constraints will also impact your choice of methods. For example, if you had to deliver a time-management program in three hours, it is highly unlikely you would be able to use a structured experience that takes an hour and a half.

Cost is another factor in the design and development of a training session. For a customer-service program, you may want to demonstrate the proper way of handling an irate customer. Doing research, you might have come across a video that would be perfect. However, a limited budget might preclude you from using it. Videos are expensive to buy or even to rent. Unless you can demonstrate that buying the video will be cost-effective because it will be used numerous times, you may find yourself searching for another means of communicating your message. (Cost issues are discussed further in Module Seven.) All is not lost, though. A less costly alternative is to write a scripted role play demonstrating the correct approach to handling an irate customer. During the training session, ask for two volunteers to read the role play, and then lead a discussion just as you would following the video. The downside is that it takes time to write the script, and it probably will be considerably shorter than the video.

MAJOR COMPONENTS OF DESIGN

An instructional plan identifies what will be accomplished *(learning outcomes for the participants)*, what will be said or presented *(content)*, and how content will be communicated *(methods and media)*. The purpose of the initial design document is to organize one's thoughts and sequence the material and activities to create the optimum learning experience and meet learning outcomes.

After determining the objectives and before writing a detailed instructional plan, it is helpful to first design or lay out the course using a design matrix. This is truly the planning phase of the developmental process.

CREATING A DESIGN MATRIX

A Design Matrix (Figure 6.1) is used to visualize the course or session. It enables you to take a broad view of what you want to accomplish and how to meet the learning outcomes. The Design Matrix provides a framework or skeleton for the course. You will then "put the meat on the bones" as you make decisions about methods and materials and prepare an instructional plan. The Design Matrix consists simply of four parts: duration, content or learning points, methods or activities, and materials or aids.

FIGURE 6.1. Design Matrix

Duration	Content/Learning Points	Methods/Activities	Materials/Aids

The Design Matrix is a rough sketch of the training session. Use it to identify and sequence content subtopics; estimate the amount of time devoted to each subtopic; consider the methods to communicate the content; and identify potential training materials and aids.

Determining Content

Content flows naturally from the learning outcomes or objectives. The important point to remember when developing or determining content is to focus on what the participants "need to know" versus what is "nice to know." This is particularly important when there are time constraints.

Many trainers new to the profession with little or no experience designing a training program ask: "Where do I start?"

Researching the Topic Unless you are a subject-matter expert, start by researching the topic, reading books and articles to gather facts and other important information. Approach the research process in much the same way you collected information for a research paper in school. In this case, however, be careful to collect information that is vital to the program, always keeping in mind the learning objectives and the "need-to-know" concept. In other words, do not go overboard collecting information. Read and distill the material. Make sure to cite sources of specific data and give credit for proprietary models. Include a full reference for every source cited, including the author's or editor's initials and last name, the title of the book (and article, if applicable), the city of publication, the name of the publisher, and the year of publication. Concentrate on recent sources—ones that have been published within the last three to five years.

Mind Mapping Mind mapping is a type of brainstorming. Often trainers have no idea where to start in terms of what specific subtopics they should include. Generate ideas related to your topic and capture them on paper by putting the title of the program in the center of the paper. Draw a circle around it to give it focus. Then just start writing down (anywhere on the paper) any ideas or thoughts that come to mind. When the ideas have stopped flowing, begin combining ideas into natural groupings, which become subtopics. Determine which are "need-to-know" and which are "nice-to-know." Decide whether to include or eliminate the "nice-to-know" topics based on time parameters. After determining the subtopics, the next step is to sequence them.

Sequencing

After you have determined the major content and learning points for the training, determine the order in which you will present the content. Now is the time to organize. Several ways can be used, depending on the type of training and what you are trying to accomplish. Although there are no hard-and-fast rules for sequencing, the following guidelines may help you make decisions about the order of content and activities.

- Start with easy activities and move to more complex.
- Use less risky activities before those that some participants might find threatening.
- Vary activities and methods in terms of length and format.
- Present easy concepts first.

Sequencing Example As a result of a mind-mapping process, let's assume that the following subtopics will be used for a one-day customer-service training session:

- Irate customers
- Internal service
- Telephone skills
- Communication problems
- Professional image
- Definition of customer service
- Personal action plan

Think about the logical arrangement of the topics and, based on knowledge of the subject, you might arrange the topics in the following order:

1. Definition of customer service

2. Professional image

3. Telephone skills

4. Communication problems

5. Irate customers

6. Internal service

7. Personal action plan

Sequencing Activity Now assume that you are going to develop a time-management program and have identified the following subtopics.

Determine the order in which you are going to address each one by numbering them from 1 to 7.

_____ Personal action plan

_____ Tips and techniques for managing time

_____ Assessing how you spend time

_____ Barriers to good time management

_____ Dealing with interruptions

_____ Overcoming procrastination

_____ Determining priorities

Approaches to Organizing Training

Present the information in a way that will maximize the learning. You want the participants to retain the knowledge *(cognitive)*, develop the skills *(behavioral)*, or heighten their awareness *(affective)*, and at the same time enjoy the learning experience.

Many of your designs will be variations of the behavior-modeling approach introduced in the 1970s by James Robinson and William Byham (Pescuric & Byham, 1996): content, positive role modeling, skill practice, feedback, and application on the job. There are, however, other ways to organize a session, depending on your intent. The following are other approaches to consider:

Sequential Sequential designs present a step-by-step process leading to a conclusion. For example, in a sales-training seminar, the content might be presented in this order: (1) establishing rapport, (2) identifying customer needs, (3) matching product benefits to needs, (4) overcoming objections, and (5) closing the sale. With this approach, the subtopics follow the pattern of the process that serves as the training focus.

Job Order This approach teaches tasks as they occur on the job. For example, a bank teller-training program might present subtopics for opening procedures in the following order: (1) taking cash drawer from vault, (2) verifying cash, (3) ordering cash, (4) logging onto the computer, and (5) preparing settlement sheet.

Priority Skill or knowledge essential to the completion of a task is taught first as a prerequisite to the training that will follow. Returning to the teller-training example, trainees would need to have knowledge about how to log onto the computer before learning how to complete other transactions.

Topical This approach addresses job knowledge in terms of topics rather than sequence of activity. Sales representatives, for example, would have to learn about the products before they could sell them; however, they would not have to learn about products in any particular order.

PURPOSE OF AN INSTRUCTIONAL PLAN

The instructional plan is a detailed guide to delivering a training program. It serves a number of purposes:

- It forces the trainer to organize material or content and present it in a logical manner.
- It identifies what materials are needed, learning points, and how content will be communicated.
- It helps you stay on track, make the points you want to make, and avoid spending too much time on a particular topic.
- In the long run, it saves time. After it is created, file it away until the next time you have to present the particular subject. Rather than "reinvent the wheel," review the plan, assemble the necessary materials, and go.
- The ability to create a detailed instructional plan will also help in your own career development. First, it gives you credibility, enhancing your image as a trainer. Second, after you have designed and developed a complete program, you will find it easier to create subsequent programs.

COMPONENTS OF AN INSTRUCTIONAL PLAN

An instructional plan consists of two parts: (1) the program overview and (2) the instructional guide.

Program Overview

The program overview details the components of the course or training session. It consists of the following:

1. *Title.* The title should be brief but descriptive.
2. *Course Description.* Identify the overall goal of the course, along with a brief description of the content.

3. *Learning Outcomes*. List exactly what the participants should be able to do as a result of this program.

4. *Length*. Give the length of the course in terms of the number of sessions, number of hours in each session, frequency, and time of day and/or day of week, if appropriate.

5. *Format and Methodology*. Describe the approach and methodology you will use, such as case studies, role plays, experiential learning activities, discussion, and so forth.

6. *Audience*. Identify who should attend (in terms of levels, job titles, or job duties) as well as group size.

7. *Participant Preparation*. If applicable, identify any pre-training assignments such as reading, completing assessment instruments, or meeting prerequisites.

8. *Instructional Materials and Aids*.

   - Document List: Handouts, transparencies, textbooks, instruments, and readings, along with the source.
   - Equipment List: Flip charts, chalkboards, overhead projector, video equipment, whiteboards, and markers.
   - Media List: Video titles (include name of producer and length of video), audiotapes, or software.

9. *Reference List*. Identify sources used in putting the program together, such as books and articles. This is particularly helpful if someone else delivering the program wants further information.

10. *Facility Check-off List*. Reminders or "To Do's" such as table setup, water pitchers and glasses, refreshments, markers for flip charts and transparencies, pointers, extension cords, and participant materials (folders, paper, pencils, name tents).

Exhibit 6.1 is an example of Part I of an instructional plan for a customer-service training program.

EXHIBIT 6.1.
Instructional Plan—Part I

1. *Title*

   Ensuring Quality Service and Customer Satisfaction.

2. *Course Description*

   To provide participants with the tools and techniques to help them enhance and fine tune their telephone customer-service skills as well as build and improve the performance of their individual work teams.

EXHIBIT 6.1. *Continued*

3. *Length*

The standard program is designed as two full-day sessions. This is subject, however, to modification based on client requirements.

4. *Learning Outcomes*

Participants will learn how to . . .

- Create a positive initial contact.
- Ensure effective two-way communication with each customer.
- Solve customer complaints effectively and efficiently.
- Handle customer complaints and difficult situations confidently and professionally.
- Develop a personal strategy for satisfying customer needs and building good will.
- Use customer-service skills in their interactions with internal customers.
- Develop a customer-focused mindset.
- Build a quality service team.

5. *Format/Methodology*

The workshop format will use interactive and experiential activities including customized role plays, case studies, group discussions, assessment instruments, and lecturettes. The exercises and activities are designed to ensure both individual and group participation.

6. *Audience*

For all employees in a primary customer-contact position. Maximum 20 participants.

7. *Participant Preparation*

Pre-session questionnaires and interviews: A questionnaire will be designed by the trainer and sent to each participant prior to program implementation. The purpose of this survey is to identify participants' perceptions of customer service and identify areas in which they would like skill development. The data collected from this will be used to develop customized role plays, case studies, and activities.

8. *Instructional Materials and Aids*

a. Document List

- Participant workbooks containing reference materials and learning exercises

- Custom-designed role plays and case studies based on participant input

EXHIBIT 6.1. *Continued*

- Various individual assessment surveys and inventories
- Simulations
- Skill practices

   b. Equipment list

- Flip chart
- Overhead projector
- VCR and monitor

   c. Media List

    Passion for Customers, CRM Films, Running Time: 25 minutes

9. *Reference List*

- Davidow, William H., and Bro Uttal, *Total Customer Service: The Ultimate Weapon,* Harper & Row, New York, 1989
- Lele, Milind M., with Jagdish N. Sheth, *The Customer is Key,* Wiley, New York, 1987
- Sanders, Betsy, *Fabled Service: Ordinary Acts, Extraordinary Outcomes,* Pfeiffer & Company, San Diego, California, 1995

10. *Facility Check-off List*

Tables:

- Facilitator: Water & glass, extension cord, course materials, markers for flip chart and for overhead transparencies
- Participants (four tables of five seats): Water & glasses, tent cards, folders, and pens
- Break Table: Coffee, tea, soft drinks, danish

Part II is the real meat of the plan. It consists of the following four parts: *time frames, content outline, training aids and materials,* and *trainer notes.* Let's take a look at each of these in detail.

Time Frames

Identify how much time each major content section takes. Indicate a time frame for each by listing the number of minutes required (e.g., 15 minutes) or express time as a digital clock (e.g., 0:15).

Content Outline

This section outlines in detail the ideas, principles, concepts, or skills you want participants to learn. There are many possible formats; however, an outline is best, as it helps you see relationships as well as the sequence of topics and subtopics. Although you do not have to worry about adhering religiously to the rules of outlining, it is important to observe some basic rules or guidelines:

- Main points and subpoints follow the order of general to specific.
- Subdivisions or subpoints must flow logically from each main point.
- Use the standard system of numerals, letters, and indentations as follows:

I. Roman Numerals

    A. Capital Letters

        1. Arabic Numerals

            a. Small Letters

                (1). Arabic Numerals in Parentheses

                    (a). Small Letters in Parentheses

- If you have a "I," you must have a "II." By the same token, if you have an "A," you must have a "B," and so forth. There cannot be just one point under a heading.

Training Aids and Materials

Training aids and materials include assessment instruments, videos, transparencies, slides, computer-generated visual aids, audiotapes, games, and evaluation tools. Include brief notations to cue you when to use an overhead projector, video, or handout. To make it easy for you (or someone else) to see at a glance what to do, use abbreviations or icons. The following are some ways to indicate your training aid without writing it out.

Training Aid	*Abbreviation*	*Icon*
Transparency	TR	
Workbook	WB	

Flip Chart	FC	
Handout	HO	
Video	V	

Trainer's Notes

In essence, trainer's notes are "stage directions" and methods. They tell you how you will communicate the content. They might include specific questions to ask the group or instructions for activities. Here are some possible "stage directions" you might choose to use:

Distribute	Write
Conduct role play	Show video
Demonstrate	Ask
Discuss	Instruct participants to
Break into subgroups	Explain

INSTRUCTIONAL METHODS

Instructional methods are the various means by which content or material is communicated. They include the use of assessment instruments; activities such as role plays, case studies, and simulations; and a host of cooperative-learning or active-training techniques (which are explored in detail in Module Seven). Some of the issues to consider when using the standard experiential methods are discussed below.

When selecting training methods, remember that there is no one best method; however, do try to use a combination of strategies. In selecting your methods of delivering instruction, consider the following:

- Subject matter
- Group's knowledge of the subject
- Training objectives
- Available time
- Group size
- Kind of participation desired
- Equipment available
- Type of room

- Cost
- Comfort zone of the trainer
- Comfort zone of the participants
- Participants' learning styles and perceptual modes (see Module Two)

Figure 6.2 lists the advantages and disadvantages of the various instructional methods. Study it to help determine which methods to use.

FIGURE 6.2.
Instructional Methods

Method	Advantages	Disadvantages
Role Playing: Acting out real-life situations in a protected, low-risk environment	Develops skills Opportunity to practice what is learned Participants gain insight into own behavior	Some participants are resistant Contrived situations Requires considerable planning
Games: An activity governed by rules entailing a competitive situation	Promotes active learning Provides immediate feedback Boosts interest Stimulates excitement Increases learning Improves retention	Time-consuming May lead to loss of facilitator control Sometimes difficult to monitor Some degree of risk
Simulations: Activity designed to reflect reality	Promotes high level of motivation and participation Provides immediate feedback Approximates real-world environment	Can be costly Time-consuming Requires significant planning and excellent facilitation skills May require more than one facilitator

FIGURE 6.2. *Continued*

Method	Advantages	Disadvantages
Observation: Watching others without directly participating; then giving constructive feedback	Generates interest and enthusiasm Is less threatening than other methods Promotes sharing of ideas and observations	Focus could easily shift from learning to entertainment Demonstrators may not do adequate job Requires skilled facilitator
Instrument: Paper-and-pencil device used to gather information	Personalized; helps to achieve participant buy-in and commitment Helps focus on most appropriate material Helps clarify theory, concepts, terminology	Some participants might be fearful Participants might argue with data Time-consuming Requires skilled facilitator Participants may feel stereotyped or "pigeonholed"
Mental Imagery: Visualizing situations; mentally rehearsing putting skills into action	Everyone can participate Stimulates thinking, imagination	Some participants may be uncomfortable or impatient No way to monitor participation
Writing Tasks: Worksheets in conjunction with materials; list and evaluate information	Everyone can participate Particularly effective for shy participant	Individual task; little or no interaction Time-consuming Some have aversion to writing

FIGURE 6.2. *Continued*

Method	Advantages	Disadvantages
Lecturettes: Short, structured, one-way communication from trainer to participants	Trainer controls what material is covered Saves time Increases participation Creates risk-free environment	Participant in passive mode May be boring to participants One-way communication
Small Group Discussion: Small groups formed from larger group; composed of 5 to 7 individuals; assigned to discuss a certain topic within certain time limit.	Stimulates thinking Draws on knowledge and experience of all group members Helps participants to assess their understanding of material	One participant might dominate No guarantee that all will participate No way to be sure everyone does understand Time-consuming Easy for group to get "off track"

When deciding which methods to use, determine your purpose. Refer to Figure 6.3 as another guide for when to use any particular method to communicate your content.

Always keep your objectives and desired outcomes in mind as you design a training session. Figure 6.4 will help you match methods to your desired outcomes.

DEVELOPING MATERIALS

Writing training materials is a time-consuming process. Not only do you have to create participant materials, but you also have to create materials for yourself—or for another trainer, if applicable. Always keep your purpose in mind. Do not get carried away trying to include everything you know about a particular subject. It is also a good idea to have someone who is unfamiliar with the topic take a look at the materials to determine if they are understandable and user-friendly.

FIGURE 6.3.
Instructional Methods—
When to Use

Method	Purpose	When to Use
Role Playing	Help participants practice skills used in interactions	• To practice newly acquired skill • To experience what a particular situation feels like • To provide feedback to participants about their behavior
Games	Provides nonthreatening way to present or review course material	• To help grasp total program content • To present dry material in an interesting way • To add a competitive element to the session
Simulations	Recreates a process, event, or set of circumstances, usually complex, so that participants can experience and manipulate the situation without risk and then analyze what happened	• To integrate and apply a complex set of skills • To elicit participants' natural tendencies and provide feedback on those tendencies • To provide a realistic, job-related experience

FIGURE 6.3. *Continued*

Method	Purpose	When to Use
Observation	Certain participants act out or demonstrate behaviors, tasks, or situations while others observe and give feedback	• To show group how to perform procedure or apply a skill or behavior • To increase participants' observation, critiquing, and feedback skills • To demonstrate behavior modeling
Instruments	Provide feedback; self-assessment	• To identify areas for improvement • To establish a baseline for future growth
Mental Imagery	Helps participants increase understanding, gain insight	• To address affective learning • To stimulate thinking, imagination • To replace role playing
Writing Tasks	Helps participants reflect on their understanding of concepts, information, ideas	• To provide for individual input

FIGURE 6.3. *Continued*

Method	Purpose	When to Use
Lecturette	Conveys information when interaction or discussion is not desired or is not possible	• To convey information quickly within short time period • To communicate same information to large numbers of people • To provide basic information to a group that is not knowledgeable
Small Group Discussions	Offers opportunity for participants to express opinions, share ideas, solve problems, interact with others	• To generate ideas • To find out what participants think about a particular subject • To increase level of participation • To encourage group interaction and build group cohesiveness
Case Study	Allows participants to discover certain learning points themselves	• To apply new knowledge to a specific situation • To practice problem-solving skills
Task Exercise or Activity	Allows participants to work with the content in small groups	• To test participants' understanding of concept or process • To promote group collaboration • To increase participants' confidence in their ability to apply learning on the job

FIGURE 6.4. Matching Methods to Desired Outcomes

Desired Outcome	Suggested Training Method
1. Knowledge	• Textbook • Lecture • Small group discussion • Games • Computer-assisted instruction • Videotape
2. Attitudes/Values	• Guided discussion • Small group discussion • Role play • Dramatization • Business games • Case study • Videotape • Simulation • Debate
3. Understanding	• Guided discussion • Small group discussion • Role play • Business games • Videotape • Computer-assisted instruction • Case studies • Demonstration/Dramatization
4. Skill Development	• On-the-job performance • Role play • Business games • Skill practice • Simulation • In-basket activity

Participant Materials

When creating participant materials, remember what you know about adult learners. First and foremost, keep in mind that you are dealing with a sophisticated audience with high expectations of the trainer, the course content, the methods used, and the materials they receive. The materials should be high quality, easy to read, and visually appealing. Also provide ample space on handouts and workbooks for participants to take notes. Workbook materials should be presented in "chunks" so that the participants can quickly and easily digest the information. To make participant materials even more useful and meaningful, include specific work-related examples. Create memory aids (called mnemonic devices) such as rhymes, acronyms, or pegging (associating words with images) to help people remember lists or important points. Create models or flow charts to present processes and procedures. Use the checklist in Exhibit 6.2 to ensure that your materials are easy to understand and use.

Participant materials also include other ancillary pieces and job aids that help reinforce learning. These take-away pieces may include checklists, pocket-sized reminder cards that list key points, or computer screen savers.

Trainer Materials

Trainer materials include the detailed instructional plan; master copies of the transparencies and participant materials; background reading; and copies of the leader's guides for videos, games, and other activities.

EXHIBIT 6.2. Checklist for a Quality Participant Workbook

_____ Headings and subheadings

_____ Bullets

_____ Boxes

_____ Short paragraphs

_____ Wide margins

_____ Graphics/illustrations/cartoons

_____ Space for note taking

_____ Exercises

_____ Checklists

_____ Conversational tone

The amount of detail in the Trainer's Guide depends on several factors:

- Who is going to use it
- The experience level of the trainer(s)
- The budget
- Amount of detail required by the key decision maker

Regardless of how elaborate the finished product needs to be, it should contain these basic components:

- Table of contents
- Introductory material providing background information
- Presentation guide that includes facilitation tips
- Instructional plan
- Master copies of handouts, participant workbook, and transparencies
- List of materials
- Resources

Before you complete the instructional plan, a number of active-training methods in Module Seven will help you create a training program that achieves the results you want.

◆   ◆   ◆

Module Seven

Selecting, Designing, and Developing Active-Training Methods

LEARNING OUTCOMES

In this module, you will learn

- To use active-training methods to increase retention, build understanding, and improve skills
- To involve all participants in the learning process
- To adapt active-training methods to any course content

THE CASE FOR ACTIVE TRAINING

Based on what we know about adult learning, learning styles, and the characteristics of today's learner (as presented in Modules One through Three), active training is the most effective means of delivering training. Research shows that people understand concepts better and retain information longer when they are actively involved in the learning process.

Active-training expert Mel Silberman, author of several books on active-training techniques, defines active training as *"the process of getting the participants to do the work."* To illustrate the active-training philosophy and its powerful impact, Silberman has developed the "Active-Training Credo," based on an old Chinese proverb (Silberman, 1998).

The Active-Training Credo

What I hear, *I* forget.

What I hear and see, *I* remember *a little.*

What I hear, see, and ask questions about or discuss *with someone else, I begin to* understand.

What I hear, see, discuss, and do, *allows me to* acquire knowledge and skill.

What I teach *to another, I* master.

This module deals with developing and selecting specific activities and materials. The module provides an in-depth look at the methods introduced in Module Six, tells where to locate materials and activities, gives some examples of active-training designs, and finally provides some guidelines for selecting and using active-training techniques in the overall design. Module Eight describes how to use these techniques.

Active Training Defined

We know from experience and through research that active training works. The active-training approach, however, requires the trainer to think through the design thoroughly. The trainer must spend time visualizing how the activity will play out, deal with logistics, anticipate participants' reactions, and identify potential problems. Active training is based on a well-researched, proven approach to learning called cooperative learning.

COOPERATIVE LEARNING

Cooperative learning is the "instructional use of small groups so that students work together to maximize their own and each others' learning" (Johnson, Johnson, & Smith, 1991). This approach to learning is based on two assumptions: (1) learning by nature is an active endeavor and (2) different people learn in different ways.

Cooperative learning is not simply putting people in pairs or groups and asking them to work on an assignment. The approach must be carefully planned and orchestrated by a skilled facilitator who composes and arranges learning experiences. Participants work in concert, encouraging and facilitating one another's efforts to achieve, complete tasks, and reach the group's goals. For this to happen, the trainer must function as an observer, advisor, coach, and consultant throughout the cooperative-learning activity.

Benefits of Cooperative Learning

The beauty of cooperative learning is that it can be used in any setting and adapted for content and individual differences. Because it focuses on individual differences, cooperative learning addresses the concerns voiced by women and culturally diverse participants, echoing the changes we are experiencing in society and the workplace. As more women and culturally diverse individuals enter the work force, managers and trainers are being challenged to re-examine old assumptions and look for new approaches for developing employees.

Cooperative learning also addresses the real-world issues of interdependence, conflict, and change. Group learning serves as an introduction to project teams and self-directed work groups found in many businesses. Organizations have found that work teams must be trained to function effectively as units.

Research Data

Research on cooperative learning began in the late 1800s. Over the past one hundred years, more than 575 experimental and one hundred correlational studies have been conducted comparing the relative effects of competitive, cooperative, and individual efforts on instructional outcomes. Studies show that cooperative learning produces higher achievement, more positive relationships among participants, and healthier psychological adjustment than do individual experiences (Johnson, Johnson, & Smith, 1991). Involving participants in the learning process results in higher-level reasoning, more frequent generation of new ideas and solutions, and greater transfer of what is learned from one situation to another. Furthermore, cooperative learning results in greater productivity.

CREATING AN ACTIVE-LEARNING ENVIRONMENT

For an active-learning environment, the instructional design should maximize the effectiveness of instruction for both the learner and the trainer.

Physical Setting

A safe, positive environment is critical to a successful learning experience. The creation of such an environment begins with the physical setting. By using music, posters, and props, the trainer creates a mood and sets the tone for the learning experience. Beginning the session with an icebreaker, opener, or other active-learning technique will help learners focus on the course content and get them involved immediately (Silberman, 1998). Other set-induction techniques such as showing a film clip or displaying a photo, artifact, or cartoon and asking participants to comment are excellent ways to build interest and prepare the participants for the learning that follows.

An integral part of the physical environment is the actual seating arrangement, which will be discussed in detail in Module Eight. Because room size and configuration are often less than ideal, it is important to determine the type of interaction desired, then arrange the seating to achieve the desired results. For example, research conducted by the 3M® Company with Wharton School of Business found that the U-shape configuration is very effective in promoting group interaction with a minimum of trainer control (Meyers & Jones, 1993).

Another way in which trainers can create a positive learning environment is to find out what participants think and feel about the subject well in advance so that this information can be used to design active-learning activities that take into account individual differences and levels of experience. This can be accomplished through pre-session surveys and phone calls to participants. On-the-spot assessment through opening activities can also help the trainer learn about participants' knowledge, attitudes, and experience (Silberman, 1998).

Strategies and Techniques

Based on learning, teaching, and motivation theories as well as research findings, primarily at the pre-college level, the following strategies and techniques appear to characterize the successful implementation of cooperative learning in an adult training environment.

Structure and Organization As noted above, cooperative learning is characterized by structured learning groups. The trainer places participants in specific groups and gives specific assignments with clear instructions and time limits. These assignments may include group tasks as well as individual roles such as recorder, timekeeper, or spokesperson. Cognizant of the different ways in which individuals perceive and process information, trainers should first form the groups to avoid confusion and then give instructions in both oral and written form by displaying them on a flip chart, a transparency, or a handout.

Moderate Level of Content Because cooperative-learning programs focus more on process than content, trainers should be guided in their design by determining what participants "need to know" rather than what would be "nice to know." Content is no longer limited to facts, dates, formulas, definitions, and so on. It has been redefined to include skills and understanding, thus ensuring a balance among the cognitive, affective, and behavioral domains of learning (Meyers & Jones, 1993). By clearly defining what participants will know and be able to do by the end of the session, trainers clarify content and select appropriate learning strategies. It is imperative that these expectations be communicated clearly to the participants at the beginning of the session, preferably before. One strategy for communicating expected outcomes is to send a memo to the participants welcoming them to the workshop and briefly outlining learner-centered course objectives and content as well as instructions for any prework.

High Level of Participation As mentioned earlier, the trainer's role is that of a facilitator whose primary function is to manage the learning process. Participants are actively engaged in activities from the start, continually involved in doing, discussing, and reflecting.

Interdependence One of the primary purposes of cooperative learning is to create interdependence among group members. In order to facilitate that outcome, the trainer requires all group members to master the content of the assignment. This might be accomplished by a jigsaw design in which the learning activity is structured in such a way that each group member is responsible for learning a specific piece of the content and then teaching it to the rest of the participants.

Minimal Lecture Although there is a place for lecture as a training method, it should be used in small doses of ten to fifteen minutes. Based on research conducted during the 1960s, lengthy, uninterrupted periods of leader-centered discourse result in confusion, boredom, and low retention (Johnson, Johnson, & Smith, 1990). Lectures, however, need not relegate participants to a passive role. Participants can be involved through various interactive techniques that promote both understanding and retention (Silberman, 1998). These techniques are addressed later in this module.

Variety of Methods "Small groups" may be used for pairs, trios, or groups of five to seven. Small groups are very effective. Not only do they incorporate all the elements of active learning, but they help develop interpersonal skills and provide those who might be reticent to participate with a risk-free environment in which to express opinions or ask questions. This helps participants gain confidence and develop the self-direction central to the adult learner.

Peer Teaching We know from our study of adult-learning theory that adults bring a wealth of experience and expertise to the learning environment. Encouraging them to draw on and share their experiences with others in the group can be rewarding for both the trainer and participants.

Iterative Process Throughout the session, the trainer uses activities that build on and overlap concepts and skills learned earlier. In this manner, learning is reinforced and participants have more opportunities to digest and integrate what they learn.

Real-World Application Through many of the methods described above, participants are able to use real-life situations when learning new concepts and skills. Sometimes the trainer solicits examples of hypothetical or real problems for the participants to use throughout the session. In addition, before the session ends, the trainer gives participants the opportunity to develop individual action plans, identifying how they are going to apply what they have learned in the real world.

DESIGNING ACTIVE-TRAINING ACTIVITIES

After you have decided on the content and have some idea of the methods and materials you want to use, the next step is to come up with specific activities or structured experiences and specific training aids.

The term "design" was used in Module Six to describe the process of planning or laying out the training session or program. "Design" is also used in conjunction with the methods and materials chosen. Each technique or activity must be carefully thought out prior to actually developing the activity.

Design Principles

As you begin to develop your activities and materials, keep in mind the following three principles:

- One design can accomplish two things at once. For example, an icebreaker can both build group cohesiveness and assess group needs.
- The same design can often be used for different purposes.
- Published designs can often be modified to suit your own needs.

Before moving on to specifics, let's address a critical issue in course development: the decision whether to use materials and activities already developed or to create your own.

Many trainers, particularly those new to the field or those faced with time and cost constraints, choose to use "off-the-shelf" training materials that they integrate into their own designs. In this module, you will learn how to select or develop individual activities, exercises, assessment instruments, and so forth.

Most trainers use a combination of developing their own, buying, customizing, and tailoring. For example, using published assessment instruments helps to maintain the integrity and professionalism of the program, providing a high degree of validity and reliability. Also purchasing simulations is wise because of their complexity and their proven success. In general, customizing or tailoring published role plays and case studies to clients' specific situations is easier and less time-consuming than writing your own.

Factors to Consider

Before jumping headlong into investigating resources for activities and materials or developing your own, consider several key factors that will influence your decision.

Time Course or program development takes time—a lot of time. Coming up with your own activities, exercises, assessment instruments, role plays, case studies, etc., can take hours, days, or even weeks. Many people are surprised to discover, however, that the process of locating the most appropriate activity or video for a given situation is also extremely time-consuming.

Cost Cost plays an important role also. If you develop your own materials, take into consideration your salary per hour as well as the salaries of any support personnel involved. Even if you select published material, factor in the cost of your research time and remember that there are costs associated with purchasing or licensing that you will incur each time you deliver the program.

Quality The quality of the materials and activities is also important. Quality can relate to the actual appearance of the materials, the credibility of the content, or the level of detail provided.

Suitability The biggest concern should be the appropriateness of the material for your purposes. Take into consideration the audience, the topic, and your objectives. Does each proposed activity or material do what you want it to do?

Trainer Experience and Expertise Also evaluate your own skills and abilities. If you want to develop your own role play or case study, for example, consider your level of creativity as well as your writing ability.

To help you decide whether to create, buy, or adapt materials, refer to Appendix C: Criteria for Selecting Packaged Programs.

COMMON METHODS AND MATERIALS

Even if you develop many of your own active-training activities, you will still need to use other sources for methods and materials such as videos and assessment instruments. In some situations you must lecture. All of these tried-and-true instructional methods, even lecture, can be redesigned to involve the participants more actively, which is discussed further in this module.

Videos

New or inexperienced trainers often develop training programs designed around videos. Videos can be very helpful for communicating a message. They appeal to visual learners and also to those who are part of the MTV generation. A video is often quite effective as a method of demonstrating skills or presenting concepts. Selecting the right video is also time-consuming, and then, of course, videos are costly to buy or rent. Ignoring the cost issue, let's look at what is involved in selecting the right video for the right situation.

Dos and Don'ts

- Keep in mind that the purpose of a video is to complement, enhance, or reinforce a message. A video is not meant to stand alone.
- Quality is very important. Today's media-sophisticated audiences have high expectations. Make sure the video you choose is not "dated" or "hokey." Participants expect a professional production.
- A training video should reflect the diversity of today's business world. The characters should not be stereotypes; they should represent a variety of races, nationalities, and ages, and have gender balance.
- Be sure the video meets your needs and satisfies your objectives. In their catalogues, video producers provide brief descriptions as well as the objectives of the videos.

Benefits

- Videos offer models of positive behavior and, therefore, they fit nicely into the behavior-modeling approach to training.
- For multiple sessions, videos help ensure that the message is consistent for all groups.
- Videos are an efficient and cost-effective means of dealing with multiple sessions and locations.
- Videos often provide the opportunity to bring well-known experts into your session.

Video Resources

There are a number of training-video producers and distributors. Some of the well-known sources are listed in Appendix B. To locate the right video for your purposes, peruse producers' catalogues or use the services of a distributor.

Direct Source If you are not receiving video producers' catalogues as yet, contact those listed in Appendix B; they will be more than happy to put you on their mailing lists. Spend time looking through the catalogues and reading the descriptions. If you find any videos that you think might meet your needs, simply contact the producer and ask to preview. The preview charge is minimal or even free; in this case all you have to do is pay for traceable return postage.

Contacting Distributors There are a few distributors across the country who represent several producers. The advantage of dealing with a distributor is that you do not have to spend hours poring over catalogues. Just call the distributor and tell the service representative your topic, the intended audience, and your objective in using the video. The distributor will recommend one or more and will also be happy to send preview copies for your review. After you have made your selection, the distributor will handle the arrangements for you to buy or rent the video. If you are lucky enough to live in a city where one of these distributors is located, you can even arrange to preview videos at their site. Many even provide free popcorn!

Whatever route you choose, be sure to preview several videos for each topic and choose the one best suited to your purpose. It is a good idea to keep records of the videos you preview to help you make your selection and for future reference. See the sample form in Exhibit 7.1 and use it the next time you preview some videos.

Instrumentation

An instrument is any paper-and-pencil device used to gather information about an individual, group, or organization. Types of instruments include surveys, checklists, inventories, questionnaires, tests, and reactionnaires. An instrument can be used to provide feedback or self-reflection and examination, identify areas for improvement, or establish a baseline or starting point for future growth.

Selecting and Developing Instruments As was mentioned earlier, assessment instruments can be purchased for a variety of purposes. For example, when addressing personality and style differences, use a personality-style

EXHIBIT 7.1. Film-
Preview Form

Film Title:

Distributor/Producer:

Topic:

Length:

Synopsis:

Uses:

Value:

Additional Comments:

profile to enable people to identify their own styles. Use it as a basis of exploring and adapting to style differences. The *Instructional Styles Diagnosis Inventory* from Module Three is an example of this type of instrument and also an example of one that does not have to be purchased individually, as it was published in one of the Jossey-Bass/Pfeiffer *Annuals* and can be copied for internal use. Others can be purchased individually.

Instruments can be used to help people gain a deeper understanding of themselves and their approaches to something. For example, the *Coaching Skills Inventory* (Phillips, 1991) can be used to identify respondents' behaviors in various coaching situations.

Questionnaires, checklists, and even some surveys are fairly easy to develop. Make them very specific to your situation. Techniques for using instruments will be introduced in Module Eight.

Selection Guidelines When selecting an assessment instrument, consider the following guidelines:

- *Validity*. Does the instrument measure what you want it to measure?
- *Reliability*. How accurate is the scoring? Does it yield the same results each time it is administered?
- *Theoretical Basis*. What is the theory behind the instrument? Does it have a sound theoretical framework?
- *Language*. Is the reading level appropriate for the audience?
- *Accessibility*. How easy is it to acquire the instrument? Can it be purchased directly from the publisher or does a distributor have to be found?
- *Fear Factor*. Could the questions or items or the reported results be intimidating or embarrassing for participants?
- *Ease of Scoring*. Is the scoring process easy? How much help will the participants need?
- *Ease of Administration*. How complex is the entire process?
- *Interpretation of Data*. How meaningful is the interpretation of the data for participants?
- *Norms/Comparative Data*. Are norms and comparative data available?
- *Time*. How long does it take to complete, score, and discuss the outcomes?
- *Cost*. How expensive is the instrument? Is it worth the investment? Can it be used again for other training events, or is it designed for one-time use?
- *Copyright*. What are the restrictions on its use?
- *Facilitator's Guide*. How complete and easy to understand is the facilitator's guide or instruction manual?

Lecture

Unfortunately, many people, trainers included, believe that training is nothing more than standing in front of a group of people with a stack of transparencies and delivering what amounts to an information dump. People seem to know intuitively from their own experience as students that lecture is not only boring but that retention is limited. So why do these same people continue to lecture?

- For one thing, lectures are relatively easy to prepare. Of course, a lot of time has to be spent in advance putting lectures or presentations together, but once that is done, it's done, and they can be used over and over.
- Another reason is that lectures save time. For those who believe that their goal is to cover vast amounts of content in a short period of time, lecture is the only way to go, with the trainer talking and the participants listening and taking notes.
- A third reason is control. It is much easier to remain in control of the situation through lecture. There is no danger of getting off track unintentionally.

Pure lecture does have its place, but a very small place in the overall training design. Sometimes lectures are needed due to time constraints or to provide certain background information. If you absolutely must lecture, deliver "lecturettes" in segments of no more than ten minutes each. One of the biggest challenges facing trainers is how to communicate cognitive material (content) without lecturing. There are some very effective ways, however, of making the lecture more interesting—and even interactive. Interactive lectures incorporate activities and involve the participants physically, mentally, or emotionally. Many are the same techniques advocated and used by professional speakers and taught in presentation-skills courses, such as:

- Question-and-answer periods
- Interesting visual aids
- Stories and anecdotes
- Case problems
- Examples and analogies

Alternatives to Lecture You may be wondering, "How do I cover all this material without lecturing? They need so much information!" Believe it or not, there are many ways to present even dull and boring information in an interesting and active way. Remember the principles and concepts from

Modules Two and Three, particularly the concept that "people learn by doing, not by being told." Cognitive information can be taught actively, using cooperative-learning techniques. Cooperative-learning designs have been used formally for decades, primarily in academic settings. Training experts Mel Silberman, Bob Pike, and Sivasailam "Thiagi" Thiagarajan have adapted, refined, and pioneered their use for a corporate-training setting.

Many active-training or cooperative-learning methods can be used in combination. Rather than being designed for use with a specific topic, most active-training techniques are "frames" that can be adapted to any content. As you design your program, look at the content and think about the different techniques that could be used to put across the information without taking an active role. There is no one right answer; it is a matter of judgment and personal preference in many cases.

Other Designs The following designs can be used to present content without lecturing. For more specific examples of the following training designs as well as ideas on presenting cognitive material in an active way, see *101 Ways To Make Training Active* (Silberman & Lawson, 1995).

Group Inquiry. Put participants in pairs to study information directly related to the course content. Ask them to study a handout containing broad information, then discuss the piece with a partner, trying to understand as much as they can, placing question marks and making notes on those things they do not understand. After a period of time, reconvene the entire group and begin answering questions the participants have generated. The purpose of this design is to arouse interest and stimulate questions. Learners raise questions as a result of their innate curiosity.

Information Search. Rather than giving information to participants, have them find it for themselves. For example, create a worksheet listing a number of questions related to the information you want them to learn. Provide resource materials such as brochures, manuals, job aids, journals, or books. Put people into pairs or small groups, give them the study sheets and resource materials, and put them to work searching for information. At the end of a designated time period, reconvene the entire group, ask the small groups to report, and discuss what they have found.

Guided Discussion. Guided discussion or guided teaching is also known as the Socratic Method. Socrates guided his students in the learning process by asking them a series of questions. With this approach, the trainer poses questions that draw on the participants' knowledge and experience and require them to think about concepts and ideas. Following cooperative-learning guidelines, pose a somewhat-broad question and ask participants to work in pairs or small groups to come up with answers.

Jigsaw Design. Choose learning material that can be broken into several parts, such as an article with several sections. Divide the participants into small groups according to the number of segments and ask each group to master one section of the text. Have each group study its material, with group members reading, discussing, and deciding how to teach the information to others. After an adequate study and preparation period, form cooperative or "jigsaw" learning groups by taking one representative from each study group to become part of a new group. Each new group then has one person who has studied each segment. Have each member of the new group teach his or her particular assigned segment to the other group members. Reconvene the large group for review and to answer questions, thus ensuring accuracy and uniform understanding. An example of synergetic learning, the jigsaw design creates interdependence among group members, who are responsible for combining separate pieces of information to create a single, coherent body of knowledge.

Learning Tournament. Divide the group into teams of five to seven people each. Give the teams time to study, discuss, and coach one another using material they have been given during the session. At the end of the study period, reconvene the entire group and distribute a handout with quiz items to each participant. Have participants complete and score the quiz individually, then have each team compute a team average. Post team scores and repeat the process. Decide how many rounds to conduct; three rounds works well. At the end of the designated number of rounds, total each team's score and award prizes to the winning team. With this design, there is individual accountability (individual quiz scores), cooperative learning (team coaching sessions), and interdependence (average team score).

Card Sort. This method is very effective for helping people learn information that has multiple sections or parts and can be easily "chunked." For example, in a session on team building, introduce participants to the four stages of team development: forming, storming, norming, and performing. Create a deck of cards consisting of four "header" cards (for the four stages) and four or five descriptors for each stage, on separate cards. Create groups of four to six people and give each group a set of shuffled cards. Instruct them to sort the cards, putting the descriptors under the appropriate headings. This is a great way for people to interact while learning information.

Experiential Learning Activities

Experiential learning means that the participants are directly involved in the learning process. They learn by actually experiencing the activity. A broad definition of experiential activities includes role plays, case studies, in-basket activities, simulations, and games. Each is addressed separately below.

Role Play The term "role play" often strikes a note of fear in the minds of even the most confident people. Role play conjures up all types of negative images and reactions, and the wall of resistance immediately goes up. Unfortunately, more than a few participants have had horrible experiences with role playing, being forced to act out or perform in front of their peers and subjected to criticism and ridicule. Embarrassed and humiliated, they vow to do everything in their power to avoid participating in role plays ever again. Others have only heard of these experiences, but the horror stories have been enough to convince them that they do not want any part of it.

The cause of bad role-play experiences is not the method but the trainer. Most problems can be traced to poor preparation and planning, as well as a lack of sensitivity on the trainer's part. To ensure that your use of role play is a positive learning experience, consider the benefits and then follow the tips for risk-free role-play experiences discussed below.

Why Use Role Play? An effective role play promotes affective, cognitive, and behavioral learning. Participants practice the skills taught, demonstrating their knowledge and understanding of the content through their application in the role-play situation. They also have an opportunity to gain insight into their own behavior.

Types of Role Plays. Several role-play options are available. The first decision is what type of role play to conduct and how to do it. Do you want to write scripts and have participants read their parts? Or do you want to create a general scenario and give each role player specific instructions that include facts about the role and how each should behave? Or you might decide to give the participants extensive detail and information about the situation, but not tell them how to behave. A fourth possibility is that the role players can create their own scenarios. The choice is yours.

Other decisions involve how you want the role play to be performed. Will role players act out the scenario in front of the room with the rest of the group observing and giving feedback? Or will people in pairs or trios role play simultaneously while a participant observes each role play? Will there be one role-play situation or several? To create risk-free role plays, try the four-part approach described below.

The approach assumes a training session that is six hours or more. It can be used with any topic to build skills or change behavior. For maximum success, design the program to include the following four types of role plays in the order presented here.

Scripted Role Play. A scripted role play is one in which the trainer writes (or buys) a prepared script and asks for volunteer participants to read their lines in front of the entire group while the rest observe. The trainer then conducts a general discussion with the entire group. This type of role play should be used fairly early in the session to demonstrate desired behavior or, if you prefer, to illustrate undesired behavior. In either case, participants should be able to identify what they should or should not do.

Coaching Role Play. A coaching role play involves both the trainer and the participants. It gives participants an opportunity to draw on the information already presented and demonstrate how well they understand the concepts and principles. In this type of role play, the trainer asks for a volunteer participant to come to the front of the group. The trainer creates the scenario and explains it to both the volunteer and the entire group. The trainer plays the role of the person whose skills are to be developed, and the volunteer plays the foil. The trainer begins the role play, stops periodically, and asks the group to tell the trainer what to say next. The trainer then takes the group's suggestions and continues the role play. The trainer repeats this stop-action technique several times and then conducts a discussion about what skills or principles were applied in the activity.

Spontaneous Role Play. A spontaneous role play is used during a general group discussion. For example, the trainer may want to communicate ways of dealing with an employee who is defensive and resistant. Instead of telling the group how to handle the situation, he or she engages in a spontaneous role play to demonstrate the appropriate approach, asking one of the participants to pretend to disagree and argue. Because this role play seems to spring from nowhere and appears so spontaneous, the participant playing the other role does not even realize he or she is role playing. A variation of this would be for the trainer to reverse roles and play the person who disagrees.

Rotating Trio Role Play. The rotating trio role play gives each participant an opportunity to try out his or her skills. This type of role play should be used near the end of the session as a means of bringing it all together. The trainer breaks the participants into groups of three. The role play consists of three rounds with three different scenarios. The participants in each trio take turns playing the primary character, who is to demonstrate the skills; the secondary character, who is on the receiving end; and the observer. Each person assumes a different role for each round. The trainer can either create the scenarios and roles or have the participants come up with their own three scenarios. If participants come up with their own, additional time must be allowed.

Case Studies A case study is a written account of a problem, generally a real situation, and how it was handled. In one approach, participants are asked to analyze and discuss how the case illustrates the learning points from the training session. In another use of case study, participants are given a written description of a situation or problem, real or fictional, confronting an individual or organization and asked to analyze the situation, evaluate alternatives, and recommend an appropriate approach or solution.

Case studies, like other experiential learning activities, enhance retention, recall, and application of knowledge in actual work situations. The sense of realism and the participation required in small groups to discuss the case create a satisfying and fulfilling experience for the participants. Case studies are used in training on management, customer service, sales, and many other human relations topics.

Case studies are more complicated than they first appear. Many participants read the case and arrive at a solution or recommendation quickly. They fail to address the most critical part of case analysis: identification of the underlying problem. Therefore, be sure to provide specific directions when introducing the activity.

As with role plays, case studies can be purchased and used as is or customized for the specific situation and organization. They can also be written, either from your own experience and knowledge of the organization and industry or by interviewing people within the organization to gather more specific details and a deeper understanding of the problems represented in the cases. Although the latter approach is time-consuming, it is well worth the effort. When participants know they are working with real-life cases, the training program has instant credibility. Because the cases are realistic and relevant, participants are more interested and eager to contribute. Cases can range in length from one paragraph to several pages, and they can also be used as the basis for role plays.

Guidelines for Writing Case Studies. The beauty of writing case studies is that you are completely in charge. Create any scenario you choose, and make the case simple or complex. The following are some guidelines for writing a case study for any topic or situation:

- *Write in story form.* Create the scenario, and then start writing what you imagine. Make it as realistic as possible.
- *Create characters.* To avoid potential problems with diversity issues, give the characters humorous names. For example, for a financial-services organization, name the characters Penny Less and Mort Gage.
- *Create some realistic dialogue.* It does not have to be much, but it makes the story more interesting and adds a sense of realism.

- *Provide specific details as appropriate.* You may or may not want to provide background information. If the details enhance the case study or provide essential information that could impact the outcome, then include it. Be careful not to include extraneous information that might detract from the main task or confuse the participants.
- *Be descriptive.* Create a picture in the minds of the participants. If appropriate, describe the physical environment or a character's emotional state.
- *Make the story easy to follow.* A lengthy or complicated case study needs subheadings. With shorter cases, the most easily read and understood are those that follow a logical sequence of events.
- *Provide discussion questions or guidelines for participants to follow as they analyze the case.* Many people, unfamiliar with this type of activity, could become confused and discouraged. Make the case challenging, but not overwhelming.

In-Basket Activities An in-basket activity is another type of experiential activity that recreates as closely as possible situations that participants would encounter on the job. These situations also include representative materials. The most common in-basket activities are used in time-management training to help participants learn how to delegate or set priorities. The trainer provides the hypothetical scenario. For example, participants may be told that they are about to leave on a two-week vacation, and all the work on their desks must be cleaned up before they go. An emergency has kept them from dealing with their in-baskets, and they now have only 30 minutes to go through the items and decide what to do with each one.

The trainer can have the participants work on the task individually or in small groups. Pairs make the activity more interesting and add the dynamic of discussion and joint decision making. The trainer distributes to each person or small group an envelope containing ten to twelve items that would typically be in someone's in-basket: phone messages, memos, letters, reports, minutes from meetings, and so forth. At the end of the designated time period—generally 30 minutes—the trainer conducts a discussion about what the participants did and why. Again, use an in-basket activity already developed or create your own. As you might imagine, writing one takes a lot of time.

Simulation For our purposes, the term "simulation" refers to lengthy, case-like scenarios that simulate problems in the work environment. The design is complicated, often requiring participants to make decisions at various points during the activity. The most well-known simulations are the consensus-seeking survival simulations used in sessions dealing with teamwork.

Business simulations also fall into this category. Generally, business simulations are tied to management or financial disciplines and address a specific skill within that discipline, such as problem solving, delegation, coaching and counseling, or planning. Unlike the survival simulations, the business simulation presents realistic management situations that test participants' knowledge and skill.

Survival simulations and business simulations are generally lengthy, requiring anywhere from one to three hours to complete and process. They are a great way to sharpen analytical thinking and task and people skills, and they help participants gain insight into their own behavior as they interact with others. Simulations are available from several publishers listed in Appendix B.

Instructional Games To distinguish games from simulations, "game" is defined here as a rule-based, competitive activity based on a defined set of goals. Instructional games are often elaborate, professionally prepared packages related to a specific topic such as customer service, diversity, or communication. Another type of instructional game is a "frame game" designed generically so that different content can be inserted and the game adapted for many different topics. Frame games based on game shows such as Jeopardy® or the ever-popular BINGO® are often used to review or reinforce content. Games are addressed in more detail in Module Eleven.

✦ ✦ ✦

Module Eight

Delivering Training

LEARNING OUTCOMES

In this module, you will learn

- To create a positive learning environment
- To use active-training techniques to gain 100 percent participation
- To set up, conduct, and process an activity for maximum learning
- To fine-tune your platform skills and stage presence

CREATING A POSITIVE LEARNING ENVIRONMENT

The success or failure of a training session is often determined long before the first participant sets foot in the training room. The trainer's job is to create and maintain an environment conducive to learning and to create opportunities for participants to experience personal growth, a sense of achievement and accomplishment, and recognition and rewards.

Much of the difference between success and failure has to do with one simple word: preparation. This includes preparing yourself and the learning environment, preparing the participants, and preparing the participants' managers.

Active from the Start or Before

Participant preparation is critical to the success of the training session. Some ways to involve participants prior to the session are covered below.

Pre-Session Questionnaire Several weeks before the session, send a letter and questionnaire to the participants. Use a letter similar to the one in Exhibit 8.1 to welcome them to the session, provide an outline of the session and logistical information, and explain anything that should be done prior to the session, such as reading assignments, self-assessment instruments, or the questionnaire.

117

EXHIBIT 8.1.
Participant Cover Letter

Dear Program Participant:

Welcome to the "Managing Conflict" workshop! I am looking forward to meeting and working with you as we explore ways to resolve conflict and prevent it from negatively impacting your business results.

In preparation for this session, please complete the following pre-session assignments:

1. "Confidential Pre-Session Questionnaire." Fax your completed questionnaire to me by Monday, November 2, 1998. My fax number is 888-555-0000.

2. "Pre-Session Assessment." Please bring your completed assessment to the session on Tuesday, November 3, 1998.

3. "Thomas-Kilmann Conflict Mode Instrument." Please complete pages 1 through 4 prior to the workshop session and bring the instrument with you on the 3rd.

It is imperative that you complete these pre-session assignments. It should take about one hour to complete all three assignments.

The session will be highly interactive, and you will have several opportunities to apply concepts and skills to "real-life" scenarios.

See you on the 3rd!

Sincerely,

Karen Lawson, Ph.D.
Program Facilitator

The purpose of the pre-session questionnaire is to find out participants' expectations and perceived needs, as well as gather information to create customized role plays, case studies, and other activities. The questionnaire helps to prepare participants mentally for the learning experience. A tip sheet can be included to help participants get the most out of the training program. This is particularly helpful for those who may be attending a training session for the first time or when the participants are coming from different locations or organizations and are unlikely to know one another. Exhibit 8.2 is a sample tip sheet. It is sent to participants from different organizations attending a three-day residential program at a conference center.

EXHIBIT 8.2. Tips for
Participants

TIPS TO HELP PARTICIPANTS GAIN THE MOST FROM "MANAGEMENT SKILLS AND TECHNIQUES"

We are committed to making this the most rewarding learning experience you have ever had. For some of you, this will be your first professional-development program; others may be attending as part of an ongoing program. In either case, we want to help you gain the most from your learning experience. To that end we offer the following tips to help you reap both personal and professional rewards.

1. This program is demanding in both time and energy. Not only will you be spending a full and active day in class, but you will also be required to complete evening assignments. To minimize your stress, we strongly suggest that you make every effort to limit personal commitments while you are attending this program.

2. Because this is an intense, concentrated program, you will not want to miss a minute of exciting activities and exhilarating class discussions. Try to arrange your travel plans so that you can take advantage of every learning moment.

3. One of the greatest benefits of a program such as this is the opportunity to share with and learn from others. So come prepared to share your needs and concerns about the challenge of managing others.

4. Take advantage of the wealth of resources in the class. Spend your time during meals, breaks, and after class networking with others—both trainers and fellow participants. Take the opportunity to talk with others about common problems and possible solutions. Your goal is to learn as much outside class as during the class itself.

5. One of the major benefits of a residential program is meeting new and interesting people. Make a real effort to avoid spending all of your time with people you already know.

6. You will discover many new ideas and techniques that you will want to apply "back home." You will want to try everything! To prevent personal frustration, plan to return from the program with a "personal-development plan" of one or two new ideas that will help improve your performance on the job.

EXHIBIT 8.2. *Continued*

7. Jump right in and become involved as much as possible when there are participative activities. You will not only learn more but have more fun too.

8. Because there are so many new things to learn, you may sometimes feel overwhelmed. To maintain focus for yourself, continually refer to the objectives of the program and ask yourself, "What am I learning?" "How can I use this on the job?"

9. Use your time well to make friends, stimulate thinking, obtain new ideas, and strengthen your own thoughts. This is what makes an enriching learning experience. You will leave the program "pumped up" and ready for action!

Pre-Session Assignments Pre-session assignments are a good way to save valuable workshop time and get participants ready for the learning experience. Keep the prework minimal—a one- or two-page reading assignment and perhaps a self-assessment instrument. Participants overwhelmed with too much will be turned off before they begin. Also, keep in mind that there will always be some people who do not complete the prework assignments. Have a plan to deal with that situation. Ask them to work on the assignment during a break or ask participants to work on the assignment while the group is involved in an activity.

Manager Involvement and Support Ideally, managers of those attending training programs should sit down with their employees and tell then how the training relates to their jobs, explain what the program is about, tell employees why they are going and what the managers expect the participants to obtain from the program, and find out what the employees hope to learn. The reality is that this does not happen very often. Although managers cannot be forced to prepare their employees for the training experience, they can be prodded a little. Send the managers a memo such as Exhibit 8.3, suggesting how they can help prepare employees for the training.

EXHIBIT 8.3. Memo to Manager

To: Participant's Manager

From: Trainer

Date: _____

Subject: Title of Training Program

Your employee, _____ , is scheduled to attend the training program entitled _____ on _____

During the program, the following topics will be addressed:

_____

_____

_____

_____

The overall goal(s) of the session(s) is/are to _____

In order for your employee to be successful in transferring learning from the classroom to the job, you, the manager, must be actively involved. Please take a few minutes to identify areas or skills you would like the participant to work on during this program. Be as specific as possible. Please share this information and discuss your expectations with the employee before the session.

Be sure to include an outline of the program and send a separate tip sheet, such as "How to Prepare Your Employees for Training" in Exhibit 8.4.

For multi-session training programs, involve the participants' managers in another way. Create "homework" assignments or projects that the participants must complete outside the sessions, discuss with their managers, and have the managers sign off on them. For example, with one or two weeks between sessions, participants can be asked to apply what they learned in the session, write a summary, discuss it with their managers, and be prepared to discuss it during the next session. Exhibit 8.5 is an example of an assignment following a session on delegation.

The more supportive and involved participants' managers are, the more positive and participative the participants are in the training session. Studies also find that the more voluntary the training, the higher the motivation and involvement of the participants.

EXHIBIT 8.4. How to Prepare Your Employees for Training

Before the Training Session

- Well in advance of the training session, sit down with your employees and explain your reasons for sending them to the program.
- Explain what the program is about, including objectives and content.
- If the employees are attending a program out of town in an unfamiliar setting, explain what they can expect. This should include a discussion of travel arrangements, lodging, and appropriate attire, along with travel-reimbursement policies and procedures.
- Tell them what you expect them to learn from the program and how the program relates to their jobs.
- Ask them what they would like to gain from the program. Encourage them to identify specific skills they would like to develop, information they want to learn, or problems they would like help to solve.
- Indicate that you will expect them to discuss the program with you when they return. You might even suggest that they write brief summaries of the learning experience, including what they learned, how they are going to use the training back on the job, and how the training will benefit them, the organization, and, if applicable, their customers. You may want them to share what they learned with their co-workers at a staff meeting.
- Employees often worry about being away from the job because of work piling up. Assure them that the work will be there when they return and not to worry about it. Emphasize that you want them to get as much out of the program as possible.

After the Training Session

- Shortly after they have returned from the training, meet with the employees to debrief.
- Ask what they learned and whether or not it met their expectations. Ask if they would recommend that others attend.
- Center the discussion on how they are going to apply what they learned. Press them to be specific, and ask how you can support them as they try to use what they learned.
- If appropriate, ask them to share their experiences, key learning points, materials, etc., with their co-workers.
- Follow up with the employees over the next few months to make sure that they are applying what they learned. After they have had adequate time to use what they learned on the job, ask them what they still want or need to learn.

EXHIBIT 8.5.
Delegation Assignment

You have now learned how to delegate. In using this skill, make sure that you:

1. Select an employee who has the capability of handling the responsibility.
2. Provide the employee with adequate training to handle the responsibility.
3. Specify the performance standards for the new responsibility.

Instructions: In the space below, outline a responsibility that you can delegate to one of your employees. Discuss it with your manager and be prepared to share it in class on _____.

Name of Responsibility:

Person to Whom You Are Delegating:

Specific Tasks to Be Done:

Performance Standards:

Your Signature _____ Date _____

Your Manager's Signature _____ Date _____

Rehearsal

Now that the up-front work to prepare participants is over, do not overlook or give short shrift to self-preparation. You must be completely comfortable and proficient with the content and the activities. Take nothing for granted. Spend plenty of time practicing. Make sure to plan transitions or bridges from one activity to another. Anticipate questions and problems and think about how you would handle them.

Seating Arrangements

In many cases, you will not have control over the room in which you are assigned to train, or even the seating arrangements. You could be stuck in a boardroom with a huge oval mahogany table and overstuffed chairs, or you might find yourself in an amphitheater with the seats bolted to the floor. Even in situations in which the chairs cannot be moved, keep in mind that people can be moved.

Different room setups result in different group dynamics. Part of the planning process is deciding how much interaction you want and how much control you want as the trainer. Then choose the seating configuration conducive to creating the desired outcome. Careful thought and planning of the seating arrangements will help facilitate participation and minimize problems.

Figures 8.1 through 8.7 illustrate common seating arrangements. Read the following seven lists indicating the trainer's intent and desired outcome. Then, referring to the figures, write down which setup will most likely achieve the desired results. Answers are given in Appendix A.

Desired Outcome One

Trainer's Intent/Desired Interaction

- Formal atmosphere
- Low group involvement
- High degree of trainer control
- Primarily one-way communication

Preferred Setup

- Seating arrangement _____

Desired Outcome Two

Trainer's Intent/Desired Interaction

- Trainer serves as facilitator
- Emphasis on small-group work
- High participant involvement
- Freedom of movement for both trainer and participants
- Room for flip chart and work table

Preferred Setup

- Seating arrangement _____

Desired Outcome Three

Trainer's Intent/Desired Interaction

- Moderate group involvement
- Trainer in control; focal point
- Allows for some participant movement
- Some two-way communication

Preferred Setup

- Seating arrangement _____

Desired Outcome Four

Trainer's Intent/Desired Interaction

- Trainer becomes part of the group
- High participant involvement and interaction
- Informal, relaxed atmosphere
- Facilitates problem solving and promotes open discussion

Preferred Setup

- Seating arrangement _____

Desired Outcome Five

Trainer's Intent/Desired Interaction

- High participant involvement
- Very informal
- Allows for changing configurations
- Conducive to a variety of activities and interactions

Preferred Setup

- Seating arrangement _____

Desired Outcome Six

Trainer's Intent/Desired Interaction

- Formal environment
- Low to moderate group involvement
- Some two-way communication
- High degree of control on part of trainer

Preferred Setup

- Seating arrangement _____

Desired Outcome Seven

Trainer's Intent/Desired Interaction

- Formal atmosphere
- Moderate participant involvement
- Trainer clearly in control

Preferred Setup

- Seating arrangement _____

FIGURE 8.1. Classroom Style

FIGURE 8.2. Horseshoe

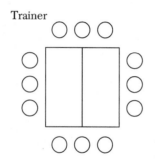

FIGURE 8.3. Single Square or Round

FIGURE 8.4. Cluster

FIGURE 8.5. Conference

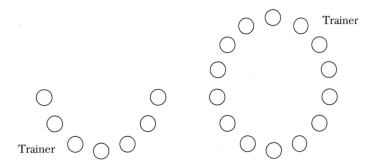

FIGURE 8.6. Semi-Circle and Full Circle

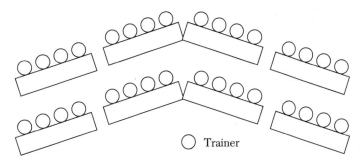

FIGURE 8.7. Chevron

It's Show Time

The importance of getting off to a good start cannot be overstated. What you say and what you do in the first few minutes can make the difference between a fabulous learning experience and a dismal failure. It is your job to (1) create a safe environment in which learning can take place; (2) stimulate participants' thinking; (3) involve the participants in the learning process; (4) manage the learning process; and (5) ensure individual participant accountability.

At the beginning and throughout the training session, you may be challenged, perplexed, and even stymied by participants' lack of motivation and sometimes outright resistance. You have, of course, taken participant motivation into account, using it as a driving force behind the design and development of your program. However, continue to be diligent and vigilant about motivational strategies throughout the delivery.

To guide you in those strategies, consider the ARCS model introduced by J.M. Keller (1983). The ARCS (attention, relevance, confidence, satisfaction) model offers an approach that ensures participant "buy-in" and participation. Use Keller's four-part model as a quality check on your design. An effective training program will reflect the following:

- *Attention*. From the very beginning, grab and hold the participants' attention, using a variety of techniques.
- *Relevance*. Design the program to meet the real-world needs and experience of the participants, and clearly point out the tangible benefits. Throughout the program, provide a framework, helping participants link content with what they already know.
- *Confidence*. Design the training and facilitate the learning process in such a way that the participants gain confidence to apply new knowledge, behavior, and skills back on the job.
- *Satisfaction*. The artful design of the training program, coupled with skillful facilitation of the process, results in a high degree of participant satisfaction with the learning experience. Additionally, the participants' ability and motivation to apply the learning results in personal satisfaction.

Grab Their Attention   The technique of grabbing participants' attention and creating a readiness for learning is called "set induction."

EXAMPLE OF SET INDUCTION

I learned (quite by accident) about set induction and the powerful attention-getting impact of a simple visual aid many years ago when I was a high-school English teacher. I was part of a three-person team teaching American literature to high school juniors. We used a large-group, small-group approach to teaching. Two days a week one of us lectured to the combined classes. Imagine 150 sixteen-year-olds in a lecture hall.

This was my first experience lecturing a large group of teenagers, and my topic was Nathaniel Hawthorne and *The Scarlet Letter*. I knew this was not exactly a hot topic for a group of sixteen-year-olds. Furthermore, having observed the behavior of the group when the other two teachers lectured, I knew I needed to come up with some way to get their attention fast.

I decided to trace a stencil of an Old English style letter "A" on a transparency and hand-color it in red. I arrived at the lecture hall twenty minutes early, put the transparency on the overhead projector, and dimmed the lights.

When the bell rang and the students came rushing and screaming into the lecture room, they stepped through the door and immediately became very quiet because all they could see was a huge red letter "A" on the screen. They began taking their seats with hushed exchanges such as "Cool," "Heavy, man," "Far out," and so forth. I had their attention immediately, and as a result I was able to conduct my lecture without the antics and disruptions the other teachers had experienced.

Using Icebreakers and Openers[1]   Techniques that immediately involve participants are very effective in piquing their interest and curiosity and preparing them for the learning experience. Many trainers start with an icebreaker, an activity designed to put people at ease and help them become acquainted. Typically, icebreakers are not necessarily related to the content. Their purpose is to help reduce tension and anxiety, energize the group, set a tone for the program, and involve everyone. Openers, on the other hand, are subject-matter-oriented activities that accomplish all the above and also introduce the participants to the session content. It is far better if the opening activity serves several purposes, including setting a tone or mind-set, and does not seem frivolous and a waste of time.

Many trainers use the tried-and-true (albeit boring) method of having people introduce themselves and say what they want to learn from the training. A variation of this method, and just as boring, is to have people pair up, interview one another, then introduce one another to the rest of the group. These two openers are not only unimaginative, but create an outcome quite the opposite from what the trainer intends. Rather than being at ease, participants are uncomfortable at having to speak up in a room full of strangers. Furthermore, with partner introductions, many people are embarrassed because they forget the other person's name or fumble with the information.

Although it is true that people should be active from the very beginning, it is also true that the activity must have a purpose beyond introducing people. To find ideas for icebreakers, browse through the dozens of books on the market that offer icebreakers, openers, and warm-up activities for every purpose. (Check Appendix B for specific titles.) Write down the ones that appeal to you and how they could be used, that is, with what topic and audience. File them for use in another session or to spruce up an existing design.

A few basic openers are included on the next few pages that can be adapted to any topic.

[1]Reprinted from Lawson, K. (1998). *Involving your audience: Make it active.* Needham Heights, MA: Allyn and Bacon.

HUMAN SCAVENGER HUNT

In programs of three hours or more, you may want participants to become acquainted quickly to establish a safe environment in which people will feel comfortable participating. One of the most popular get-acquainted activities that also guarantees instant involvement is the "Get-Acquainted Scavenger Hunt" made popular by John Newstrom and Ed Scannell (1983).

Instructions: Prepare a sheet on which you ask participants to "find someone in the room who. . . ." and then list a number of descriptive statements. Ask participants to circulate around the room and find people who fit those criteria. When a person fits a particular criterion, ask that person to sign his or her name. Any individual can sign another person's sheet only once.

The following scavenger hunt, adapted from Scannell and Newstrom's (1983) activity, could be used for a session on time management.

Find someone in this group who . . .

• Has been told he/she is a good cook _____

• Uses a daily planner or "to-do" list _____

• Schedules his/her day the night before _____

• Was born in the same month as you _____

• Maintains a neat desk or work area _____

• Listens to educational tapes _____

• Has more than two pets _____

Notice that the statements are either content-related or personal. Content questions include those that address having a daily "to-do" list, maintaining a neat work area, listening to educational tapes, and scheduling the night before. Personal items include cooking, pets, and birthdays. The two types of questions give participants an opportunity to relate on a personal level, while preparing mentally for the session content.

THE PARTY

This activity is great for networking and becoming acquainted. It creates movement and enables people to meet a number of fellow participants, regardless of the group size. The topics discussed can be adapted to any content.

Instructions:

1. Prior to the activity, hang or display posters on the wall or on easels around the room related to both the theme of the session and the topic. For example, use movie posters for a movie theme in a session on conflict, leadership, communication, or almost any subject. To make the theme more specific, use any type or category of movies, such as Disney films, science fiction, horror, westerns, musicals, comedies—the possibilities are endless. For a zoo theme in a diversity program, post large pictures of different zoo animals. Posters representing different sports (football, tennis, golf, basketball, soccer, hockey, or skating) or perhaps teams within a particular sport would work well for a sports theme and for team building.

2. Tell participants to look around at the posters and select their three favorites. Explain that there will be three rounds of groupings or gatherings. During Round One, they are to go to the designated area for their first choice; Round Two, their second choice; Round Three, their third choice. Tell them how long they will have for each round.

3. After the subgroups are formed for the first round, ask the participants to discuss the questions or topics that appear on their instruction sheets or flip-chart sheets for that round.

Sample Rounds

Round One

- Introduce yourself to other members of your group by stating your name, where you live, and your position and responsibilities.
- Explain briefly why you selected this particular [movie, animal, sport, etc.] as your favorite.

Round Two

- Identify something you have in common with the other members of your group. Some possible topics might include hobbies, sports activities, family, pets, or job.

Round Three

- "What are your concerns or expectations for this session?"

4. After each round, the facilitator will process the activity by selecting participants at random to respond to the following questions:

- Round One: "Who in your group traveled the farthest to attend this session?" "Why did you choose this [movie, sport, team]?"
- Round Two: "What did you find in common?"
- Round Three: "What were the major concerns or expectations in your group?" "What was the most interesting thing you learned through this activity?"

This activity can also be used at any time during the session by making the questions content-specific. For example, in a change-management program, ask the following:

- Round One: "What changes are you experiencing in your organization?"
- Round Two: "What is the impact of change on employees?"
- Round Three: "What is the impact of change on you as a manager?"

GETTING AROUND

Instructions:

1. Put four content-related questions (or unfinished statements) on a flip chart or transparency. Show only one at a time. For example, for a workshop entitled, "Managing Change and Stress," post these four items:

   • It is important to manage stress effectively because. . . .
   • Some reasons people resist change are. . . .
   • Some of my strengths in managing stress are. . . .
   • I know I would be healthier if I. . . .

2. Ask participants to stand up, pair with someone they do not know (or do not know very well), and discuss the first statement or question for a few minutes. (Be specific about how much time they have.)

3. Call time. Then ask participants to pair up with someone different (again, someone they do not know well) and discuss the next item.

4. Continue until all four items (four rounds) have been discussed. If time is short, use only three rounds.

5. Discuss in the total group what the participants learned from this activity.

ACTIVE KNOWLEDGE SHARING

When trainers cite some interesting facts or statistical information about a subject, participants' reactions can range from genuine interest to polite attention to glazed eyes. Rather than giving participants the facts and figures, use an activity called "Active Knowledge Sharing" (Silberman & Lawson, 1995). Ask participants to work together in twos or threes and make an educated guess about the facts or statistics. Then show a prepared slide, transparency, or computer screen on which you have provided the factual statement with the number or percentage to be filled in by the participants. For example, in sessions dealing with listening skills, present the information using the following format:

- A speaker can speak at a rate of _____ words per minute; we can hear at a rate of _____ words per minute.
- On the average, we spend _____ percent of our waking hours communicating; _____ percent of that time is spent listening.
- People learn _____ percent by sight; _____ percent by listening; and _____ percent by all other senses combined.

If the participant group is small (20 to 25), go around the room and ask people to quickly give their figures and write them on a flip chart or an overhead transparency. If the group is large, ask a few people at random to share their figures. Then show the correct information. Participants really enjoy this activity. It takes very little time, yet piques their interest and curiosity. They are motivated to listen because they want to find out if they were correct. It is important to have people work together so that no individual is put on the spot and to create a safe environment for audience members. People are much more likely to remember these facts and figures because they were directly involved.

INSTANT ASSESSMENT

Another activity that gets people involved from the beginning is called an "Instant Assessment" (Silberman & Lawson, 1995).

Instructions: Prior to the session, prepare sets of different colored 3" x 5" cards. Each card set should consist of four different colors, each with a different letter (A, B, C, and D) on it in large letters. Give each participant a set of cards. Begin by telling the participants that you would like to find out a little more about them so that you can address their specific needs. Tell them to indicate their answers to some questions by holding up the card that corresponds to their response. Display the questions one at a time on the overhead projector, giving participants time to respond to each item. Ask a few people to explain their choices.

For example, for a session on influencing others you might use the following items:

- My main motivation for attending this session is
  A. To escape from the office
  B. To learn how to increase my personal effectiveness
  C. Because my boss made me
  D. I have no idea why I'm here

- When giving feedback, I believe you should
  A. Be blunt and to the point
  B. Cushion the negative between positive statements
  C. Describe specific behavior
  D. Address the person's attitude

- When faced with a conflict situation, I
  A. Ignore it and hope it will go away
  B. Hold firmly to my position
  C. Give in with little resistance
  D. Beat the other person into submission verbally

- Which of the following words do you most closely associate with the word *influence*?
  A. Power
  B. Authority
  C. Compel
  D. Persuade

People really enjoy this activity. It takes little time, yet gets people immediately involved in the content of the session. Notice that the items have an element of fun to them, yet also have a serious content-related component. This activity also appeals to people who are tactile because they have an opportunity to touch and pick up the cards. From the trainer's point of view, the responses reveal some interesting information that can be referred to throughout the session.

WHAT DO YOU WANT TO KNOW?

Instructions: Prior to the start of the session, prepare flip-chart sheets with the major subtopics as headings, one subtopic per sheet. Post the pages on the wall. At the beginning of the session, give each participant a pad of Post-it™ Notes. Ask them to look at the topics and write down any questions they have about any or all of the topics. They may write as many questions as time permits (you set the time limit), but may put only one question per Post-it™ Note.

After they have written their questions, they are to stand up and place the Post-it™ Notes on the appropriate flip-chart sheets. Rearrange and group similar questions, followed by comments linking the questions to the session content. Occasionally participants will post questions unrelated to the session. This is a good opportunity to clarify expectations by pointing out what will and will not be addressed.

PRETEST

At the beginning of a session, have participants complete a quick quiz related to the content. This technique not only raises the participants' interest level but also establishes the purpose of the training session. For example, the following are questions you might ask about writing business letters:

True or False:

1. It is acceptable to abbreviate the month when typing the date on a business letter.

2. In business letters, when the salutation consists of only a first name, it is acceptable to use a comma, e.g., "Dear John,".

3. When using full block style, the complimentary close should be flush with the left-hand margin.

4. When writing a letter to a company, if you do not know the names of the people to whom you are writing, you may use "To Whom It May Concern."

5. When addressing more than one individual, place the names on separate lines in alphabetical order.

This type of quiz creates awareness among participants that they may not know as much as they thought they did about the topic, and that recognition motivates people to "buy" what the trainer is "selling."

A quiz or self-evaluation can be handled in one of two ways. One approach is to have people complete and score the quiz individually. Another is to ask participants to work on it with a partner. Working in pairs is less threatening and serves to generate interest and enthusiasm as the pairs discuss and debate their answers.

What's in It for Them   Participants attend a training session for a variety of reasons. Some really are excited and cannot wait to start; others view the experience as worse than a trip to the dentist. Some cannot imagine why they are there. After all, they have "been there, done that."

Although it is true that people come to sessions with a lot of "baggage" you do not know anything about and cannot do anything about, you can lessen their resistance and improve their general mind-set by pointing out "what's in it for them." Tell them how this session will benefit them by enhancing their skills, providing them with additional information, or helping them overcome any barriers that might be preventing them from doing their best—how the training will improve their lives.

Preview of Coming Attractions   After explaining the benefits to them and providing any background as to why and how this program came about, review the objectives by comparing intended outcomes with their needs and expectations. Several of the opening activities mentioned earlier, such as "What Do You Want to Know?," are very effective for making sure both trainer and participants are on the same page from the very beginning.

Be sure to provide an overview of the program, including your expectations, time frames, break times, and logistics. Let the participants know, for example, how often and how long the breaks will be, as well as how you are going to monitor and signal when breaks are over. This is also the perfect opportunity to explain the interactive format, particularly for those who have only experienced trainer-centered, passive learning.

EXPERIENTIAL AND ACTIVE-TRAINING TECHNIQUES

After the opening activities are over, it is time to move to the meat of the program. Introduce the first activity. If you follow your carefully crafted design, you should have no problem. Not necessarily! The design may look great on paper, but how it plays out is what is important. Many trainers design and develop what appears to be a dynamite session, with plenty of participant interaction. If the session fails, they blame the participants ("What a bunch of losers!"); others denounce the use of participant-centered, active-learning methods and revert to the comfortable and less-risky trainer-centered approach.

Using Small Groups

Participants will be in small groups for most of the activities you will be conducting. The ideal size for a subgroup is five to seven people. The minimum is three, with eight as the maximum. Sometimes, however, participants will be working in pairs. Small groups, by definition, include pairs and trios. Pairs provide intimacy and thus instant interaction. Trios have the advantage of offering multiple views on the problem being discussed. "Buzz group" is another term for small group, from the "buzzing" sound of multiple groups engaged in lively discussion.

If possible, arrange for break-out rooms for small-group activities. Putting subgroups in separate rooms saves time, is less noisy, and preserves a collective spirit. Unfortunately, it is not always possible to have separate rooms. If that is the case, carve out areas within the main room and form small-group clusters with as much space between them as possible.

Assignments to small groups typically assume the form of a question or problem. Or ask small groups to develop a list, share personal incidents, or produce a definition.

The Power of Two

So far we have addressed methods and activities that involve the entire group or a number of small groups, but do not overlook the power of pairs to promote active learning. Asking participants to work with learning partners is an efficient and effective cooperative-learning technique. It guarantees 100 percent participation; as Mel Silberman puts it, "People can't hide or be left out in a pair." Pairing not only promotes interaction, but also creates a safe environment in that no individual feels pressured to come up with the right answer.

Experiential Learning Cycle

For activities to do what they are designed to do, the trainer must make sure each activity completes the Experiential Learning Cycle.[2]

Experiential learning is a process by which participants learn inductively, that is, discover for themselves the intended learnings through direct experience during an activity. The Experiential Learning Cycle is a model of the five-step process that enables the participants to learn or derive meaning from what they experienced. This model is represented in Figure 8.8.

- *Experiencing.* The process starts with participants experiencing or becoming involved in an activity. The basis for the entire process, the experience itself requires participants to do, say, hear, observe, etc.
- *Publishing or Sharing.* Following the actual experience, participants share their reactions to and observations about the activity.

[2]From Jossey-Bass/Pfeiffer's *Reference Guide to Handbooks and Annuals,* 1997 edition. San Francisco: Jossey-Bass/Pfeiffer.

FIGURE 8.8.
Experiential Learning
Cycle*

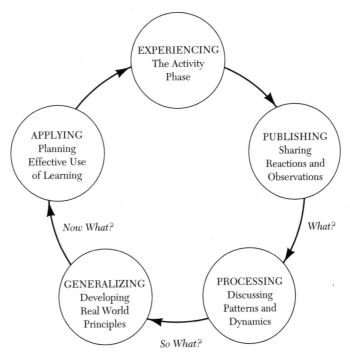

*Source: From Jossey-Bass/Pfeiffer's *Reference Guide to Handbooks and Annuals*, 1997 edition. San Francisco: Jossey-Bass/Pfeiffer.

- *Processing or Interpreting*. In this part of the cycle, the trainer helps participants address the dynamics of the group interaction. During this critical stage, the facilitator helps the group explore and analyze what happened to them during the experience.
- *Generalizing*. After processing, participants make a connection between the activity and their real-world situations. They explore the meaning of the activity and how it relates to them. This is where most experience an "AHA!" The light bulb goes on. The participants reach a deeper level of understanding and insight.
- *Applying*. The final step requires participants to think about what they are going to do with their new learning, how they are going to apply it.

If any part of the cycle is omitted or inadequately addressed, there is a high probability that the structured experience will not produce the desired results. In fact, the processing and subsequent parts of the cycle are where the real learning takes place. Therefore, plan carefully and allow sufficient time for complete processing of the activity. As a rule of thumb, spend as much time on processing—that is, discussing the activity—as you spend on the activity itself.

With that in mind, take a look at the following systematic process for managing each experiential learning activity.

Introducing the Activity

All training activities, including role plays, case studies, assessment instruments, small-group discussions, and other structured experiences, must be introduced or positioned within the context of the overall session. Here are some guidelines for introducing any experiential learning activity:

- Give the purpose and objectives for the activity. Be careful not to give out too much information. If you are focusing on discovery learning, then do not tell the participants what they are supposed to learn from doing the activity. That would defeat the purpose of inductive or discovery learning.
- Rearrange the furniture and regroup the participants as appropriate for the activity. The goal is to group people as quickly and as efficiently as possible.
- Provide specific instructions as to what the participants are to do both during and after the activity. Define terms and distribute materials, carefully going over printed material. It is a good idea to write and display on a flip chart a brief, step-by-step outline of the activity, including times associated with each step. For example, the time line for a survival simulation might look like this:

2:00	Individual reading	10 minutes
2:10	Individual ranking	15 minutes
2:25	Group discussion	25 minutes
2:50	Group ranking	15 minutes
3:05	Scoring and posting	10 minutes
3:15	Discussion of activity	40 minutes

- Make sure all participants are settled in their small groups *before* giving them any instructions or explanations. People have a hard time concentrating on two things at once.
- Make appropriate role assignments. To help pace the group on longer assignments, have each small group appoint a timekeeper. If small groups must write something on flip-chart sheets, they will need a scribe or

recorder. If each small group must report back to the large group, tell each to appoint a spokesperson. Make it clear that you do not want the same people assuming the same roles each time.

- Solicit questions and make sure everyone understands what they are to do before continuing.
- If necessary, demonstrate any rules or procedures.
- Begin the activity and circulate around the room to each small group to determine if everyone knows what to do. Clarify as needed.

Conducting the Activity

Even though the participants are engaged in the activity, the trainer still has work to do. The following are some guidelines for keeping the activity on track:

- In the first few minutes of the activity, expect some confusion and/or frustration. It's okay. Some of this helps encourage problem solving and learning. Remember that the participants are learning by doing.
- Continue to move about the room from group to group to make sure the participants are on track.
- Remain in your role as the facilitator. Resist giving participants the answers or becoming directly involved in the activity. Give suggestions or ask guided questions, if you find that participants are way off the mark.
- Continually observe how individuals and small groups are working on the task or problem, as well as how the members work together. Intervene only when absolutely necessary!
- Remind the participants of time passing, giving them signals half-way through a particular stage and also two-minute warnings for each deadline.
- Use your judgment about calling time. In some cases, you may have to allot extra time; in other situations, the small groups may finish earlier than anticipated and be ready to move on to the processing stage.

Processing the Activity

What happens after the actual activity is over is critical. For our purposes, "processing" the activity refers to the entire discussion of the activity and includes the next four stages of the Experiential Learning Cycle: publishing, processing, generalizing, and applying.

- Remember that this is where the real learning takes place. Plan to use about as much time to process an experiential activity as it took to conduct it.

- If you used only some of the participants to do a demonstration or role play, elicit feedback from them first before eliciting it from others.
- To make sure you address each part of the Experiential Learning Cycle, prepare questions using the following format: What? So what? Now what?

    - Begin by asking participants *what* they experienced during the activity: "What went on during the activity?" "What was your reaction?" "What did you observe?" "How did you feel?"
    - Next ask questions that address *so what*? "What did you learn about yourself?" "What did you learn from the experience?" "What similar experiences have you had?" "How does this relate to anything you have experienced on the job?" "How did this experience help you?" "What are the implications of the behaviors you experienced or observed?"
    - Finally, ask participants to answer questions dealing with *now what*? "How can you apply what you learned on the job?" "What might you do differently?" "How can this experience help you in the future?"

- Record participants' feedback and points on the flip chart. Ask one participant to serve as a scribe so that you can concentrate on facilitating the discussion.
- Do not be alarmed if people have differences of opinion. That is quite healthy. Just make sure the discussion does not get out of control.
- Be sure that you have completed the learning cycle and helped participants make the connection between the activity and their own situations.
- Wrap it up by asking a few general processing questions to elicit feedback and reactions to the activity itself.

    - "What did you like about the activity?"
    - "What did you dislike about the activity?"
    - "What changes would you make?"
    - "What suggestions do you have to make this a more meaningful experience?"

- Do not worry about hearing some negative reactions. Every participant cannot be expected to like every activity. Negative reactions are prompted by many factors, including learning style. Do not agonize over one or two negative comments. However, if the entire group reacts negatively, do some real soul searching and take a careful look at the design, as well as your facilitation.

Creating Your Own Activity

Think about something you would like to communicate to participants. Then decide on an activity or specific method that will actively involve the participants in learning the material. Using the worksheet in Exhibit 8.6, think through and then outline the entire process for the activity, including specific processing questions.

EXHIBIT 8.6. Creating an Activity

Name of Activity _____

_____

Participants _____ Group Size _____

Objectives/Purpose for This Activity _____

_____

Type of Training _____

_____

Time Needed_____ Room Setup _____

_____

Supplies/Equipment _____

_____

Materials/Handouts _____

_____

Directions for Activity _____

_____

Introducing _____

_____

Conducting _____

_____

EXHIBIT 8.6. *Continued* Processing (include specific questions) _____

_____

_____

Variations _____

_____

_____

Resources _____

_____

_____

Notes _____

_____

_____

TIPS FOR USING SPECIFIC METHODS

Although the steps and guidelines just mentioned are appropriate for any method, it is important to address some special considerations and guidelines related to specific techniques.

Assessment Instruments

Like other activities, assessment instruments need to be properly introduced and positioned. This is particularly important with self-assessment instruments that some participants might find threatening. Consider the following guidelines for the use of assessment instruments:

- Begin by explaining what the assessment is designed to do and why you have chosen this one in particular.
- Emphasize that this is an assessment, not a test. A test implies that there are "right" and "wrong" answers. Point out that there is no right or wrong answer.
- Explain thoroughly how participants are to respond to the assessment items. It is a good idea to read the instructions aloud and also demonstrate, using a transparency, how to mark the responses. This, of course, depends on the complexity of the instrument.
- Give participants adequate time to complete the instrument, but let them know how long it should take.
- After they have completed the instrument, ask them to put it aside until everyone is finished.
- At this point, you may want to present a lecturette or engage participants in an activity that introduces them to the theory behind the instrument and the topic.

- After participants have an understanding of how the instrument relates to the topic and what the assessment is designed to show, ask them to predict what their scores might be. For example, the *Thomas-Kilmann Conflict Mode Instrument* (Xicom, 1974) is designed to give participants insight into their approaches to dealing with conflict. After they complete the instrument and put it aside, introduce them to the five approaches using a card-sort activity. Then ask them to write down which approach they tend to use most frequently. (Most people believe they primarily use collaboration, when, in fact, collaboration is the least-used approach.)
- After the participants have written down their predictions, ask them to score the instrument and read the interpretive material.
- Then conduct a discussion to clarify the participants' understanding of the assessment and what the scores mean. Ask for volunteers to share their scores and personal insights. Ask people to indicate if their scores were consistent with what they expected. In other words, did the data confirm or refute their speculations? If people disagree with the results of the assessment, point out that they generated the data, and only they can verify it. Suggest that they revisit particular items that caused them concern and analyze their responses.
- The last step, of course, is to process the activity using the general suggestions and guidelines discussed earlier.

Videos

Participants often regard videos as an opportunity to "take a snooze"—sometimes literally. How the video is used is critical to the success of this method. Follow these suggestions to ensure maximum impact:

- Introduce the video by explaining why you are showing it and what the video is about, including a brief description of the setting and characters. Also, prepare participants for anything unusual or unique in the video. For example, any of the videos produced by Video Arts reflect the British accent and dry wit of actor John Cleese.
- Tell the participants what to look for as they view the video. In fact, it is a good idea to prepare a list of specific questions related to the video and create a handout or post the questions on a flip chart. The entire group can address each question or different questions can be assigned to specific individuals or groups of participants. This technique will make the participants much more attentive because they know they will have to report their observations to the entire group.
- Show the video in its entirety; then lead a discussion based on the questions or points the participants were to look for.

- Use the stop-action technique. This involves stopping the video at strategic places to discuss points or observations. Studies show that the stop-action technique results in significantly greater learning. Here are three ways to use film-stopping intervals:

  - Ask the group, "What would you do?" to give the participants an opportunity to speculate on what they believe is the most appropriate action or behavior.
  - Ask the participants to recap or review the key learning points they saw demonstrated in the segment just viewed.
  - Ask them how the video segment relates to their own situations on the job.

- Whichever viewing method you choose, make sure to devote adequate time to processing, just as you would with any other activity or technique.

Role Play

As discussed earlier, role plays are extremely effective if handled properly. Keep in mind the following guidelines when using any type of role-play activity:

- Be clear about your objectives and communicate them clearly to the participants. Be sure they understand that the purpose is to practice the skills they have learned in the session.
- A risk-free environment is critical to the success of a role play. The key is to introduce role plays incrementally and only after you have presented a model of desired behavior through a video or demonstration.
- Review the procedure, steps, or skills that have been presented throughout the session.
- Prepare an Observer Sheet that helps the observer focus on each role player's behavior. This sheet can also serve as a checklist for the participants to follow after the session is over.
- Hear feedback first from those who participated as actors and then from observers before giving your own input.
- During the discussion, maintain focus on the process, not the content.

Simulation

Because of its length and complexity, simulations require more time and thought when preparing the participants. In addition to following the general guidelines for introducing, conducting, and processing an activity discussed earlier, be sensitive to the potential risks. Because participants are in small groups, they will interact with a smaller number of people for a lengthy period. These factors, coupled with the nature of the activity, are likely to create more stress among individuals as they deal with both task and people skills. People tend to "show their true colors," which sometimes results in intragroup conflict. Do not be surprised when it happens, and use it as a learning opportunity during the processing stage.

Storytelling

Do not overlook the power of telling stories to illustrate points throughout your training session. People love to hear real-life accounts of events. Such accounts make the session come alive and lend credibility to the training.

IMPROVING PLATFORM PRESENCE

How you come across to participants is just as important as your training design and content. In fact, because you are the medium through which the message is communicated, your demeanor, appearance, and behavior can make or break a program.

Physical Appearance

People form an impression of you within the first few seconds—as soon as you enter the room. That impression is lasting and often determines how participants react to you.

Three words should guide you in your selection of dress for training sessions: *professional, appropriate, comfortable.* First and foremost, remember that you are a professional, and that is the image you want to project at all times.

A good rule of thumb is to dress equal to or above the level of your training group. If, for example, your participants are dressed in business casual, then you, too, should dress accordingly, but go one step beyond a skirt or slacks and a sweater. Add a blazer or sport coat. Above all, make sure your clothing is comfortable and fits well.

Avoid wearing anything distracting. This is a particular concern for women and their accessories. Do not wear bangle bracelets or dangling earrings; both become a distraction rather than an enhancement. Shoes are another consideration. Men's choices are limited—slip-ons or tied. The choice is determined by the degree of casualness of the rest of their attire. Women, however, can choose flats or heels of varying height. This becomes a matter of personal preference and comfort. Particularly when conducting an all-day seminar or workshop, do not wear very high heels. They change the center of gravity, cause you to walk and stand differently, and do not provide the stability and balance needed in front of a training group.

EXAMPLE OF CLOTHING'S EFFECT

Never underestimate the effect your clothing and appearance can have on a group. I experienced this firsthand when, at the end of a one-day session, a participant gave me extremely low marks on an evaluation sheet, noting that I had worn a red suit. He also complained to the program director about the red suit. The program director remarked that she had advised me to wear bright colors because I was training in a very large tiered lecture hall and standing against a black background. The participant would not be swayed. He had learned somewhere that red is an aggressive color and was put off by it. In another session, a participant reacted negatively to my eye makeup and noted it on an evaluation.

Body Language, Gestures, Movement, and Facial Expression

Body language, gestures, movement, and facial expression all contribute to the impression participants form of you. They can either encourage participants to listen or discourage them from paying attention to your message.

Posture   Always stand straight with your feet shoulder width apart to give you balance. If you stand with your feet close together, you will have a tendency to sway. Of course, in an all-day training session, you may become less formal and sit on a table or with the participants later in the day. So much depends on the group, the topic, the organization's culture, and the mood you are trying to create.

Gestures   Gestures are very effective means of emphasizing points. They should be natural, meaningful, and controlled. Do not fling your arms wildly or use your hands and arms in a robotic manner. When you extend your arm and hand in a pointing gesture, be sure to keep your fingers together, using your entire hand to point rather than one finger. Remember that sharp, sudden gestures create negative emotions.

Movement   Although movement is a matter of style, be aware of the impact it can have on a group. At one extreme is the statue, the trainer who stays in one place and never moves. Although certainly not distracting, this posture is not interesting. At the other extreme is the trainer who is in constant motion, who never stays in one place for more than a few seconds. Not only is this behavior distracting, but participants will probably feel worn out or exhausted by the end of a session just from watching the trainer.

Facial Expression Do not overlook the importance of facial expressions. From the first moment the participants see you, they should feel your warmth. The most effective way of achieving this is to smile with both your mouth and your eyes. Throughout the session, your facial expressions can help or hinder your message. Make sure your expressions are congruent with your words. Do not frown if you are saying something meant to be positive and upbeat.

Remember: What people see is more powerful than what they hear. Perception is reality, and how participants perceive you will impact not only how they react to you personally but how they react to the learning experience.

◆ ◆ ◆

Module Nine

Using Visual Aids

LEARNING OUTCOMES

In this module, you will learn

- To use visual aids to enhance training and improve retention
- To achieve maximum impact with visual aids
- To create various visual aids

RETENTION RATE IN VISUAL LEARNING

Visual aids play an important role in helping participants retain information; however, they should never take the place of good training. Research shows that people can retain only one to five pieces of information. That means that you must find ways to increase that retention rate.

Before exploring other reasons for using them and giving specific examples, let's take a look at the research supporting the use of visual aids. The 3M® Company has sponsored two studies, one with the Wharton School's Applied Research Center (Oppenheim, 1981) and one with the University of Minnesota's Management Information Systems Research Center (Vogel, Dickson, Lehman, & Shuart, 1996), to look at the impact of visuals (primarily overhead and computer-generated visuals) on business presentations and meetings. The results of these studies support the widely held belief that visuals do indeed increase retention and effectiveness.

The Wharton study found that presenters using overhead transparencies were perceived as more polished and professional. They came across as better prepared, more persuasive, more highly credible, and more interesting (Oppenheim, 1981). Results from the University of Minnesota 3M® Study showed that when visuals were added to an oral presentation, retention was

Note: This module is taken from Lawson, K. (1998). *Involving your audience: Make it active.* Needham Heights, MA: Allyn and Bacon.

increased by about 10 percent and the presentation became more than 43 percent more persuasive. Furthermore, presenters using computer-generated visuals were perceived as being more concise, more professional, clearer, more persuasive, more interesting, and more effective in the use of supporting data (Vogel, Dickson, Lehman, & Shuart, 1996).

Researcher Edgar Dale developed what is now known as "Dale's Cone of Experience" (Walters, 1993). His studies conclude that people will remember

- 20 percent of what they hear
- 30 percent of what they see
- 50 percent of what they see and hear
- 80 percent of what they see, hear, and do

Why Use Visual Aids?

The main purpose of visual aids is to enhance the training and to improve retention. The key word is *aid*. Visuals should not take the place of the spoken word. After all, if the visual can stand alone, then the trainer is not necessary.

To Capture Attention Visual aids help capture and keep the participants' attention. A visual aid can be extremely simple and even somewhat primitive, or it can be slick and dramatic. It all depends on personal choice, cost, available resources, type of presentation, room size and setup, audience, and purpose.

To Reinforce Points Visual aids also reinforce the points being made. With key words or graphics, the message is communicated both visually and verbally. As noted earlier, the likelihood that the message will be retained increases from 20 percent to approximately 50 percent.

To Organize Information Visual aids help to organize material. They help keep you on track and ensure that all the information is covered. Keep in mind, however, that the visual aids do not drive the training session. The trainer has already developed the program and the training materials, and the visual aids are placed strategically within that framework to enhance the program.

As a tool for organizing, visuals are also a way for the trainer to guide the participants. If the trainer uses a visual to present each key point, the participants are better able to follow the organization of the session. As a result, the trainer appears more professional, looks better prepared, and comes across as more competent.

To Promote Understanding The use of visual aids promotes understanding. They illustrate the spoken message with graphs, charts, pictures, or key words. This is particularly valuable if the trainer is explaining concepts or somewhat complex information. For example, the trainer might be making a presentation involving a lot of figures and statistics. The information will be more interesting and meaningful if it is presented on charts and graphs, rather than in rows and columns of numbers.

To Support the Spoken Message Visual aids support the message by stimulating the participants' senses. Easy access to computer-generated graphics enables trainers to enhance their messages with interesting colors, pictures, motion, and sound.

To Emphasize Key Points Although various verbal techniques may be used to emphasize key points, many participants may not be attuned to the trainer's use of emphasis. For example, the trainer may say something like, "The first important point is . . ." or "I can't stress enough the importance of . . ." or "Now that we've addressed the causes, let's look at the effects." Keeping in mind that most people are not good listeners and that people process information through different modes, putting the key points on a visual helps place the emphasis where the trainer intends it to be. There should be no doubt about the importance of information that is displayed visually.

Guidelines for Using Visual Aids

Regardless of which visual aid you use, the following guidelines will help you to create visuals that obtain the results you want.

Limit Their Use First, do not use too many visuals. Some so-called training sessions are nothing but one screen, slide, or transparency after another. Keep in mind that the visual is an *aid,* not the entire presentation.

Keep It Simple Nothing is more annoying than looking at a transparency made directly from a page of text crammed with uninterrupted lines of information. Put only one idea on each visual and no more than one illustration. There should be only six or seven words per line and six or seven lines per visual. Some trainers who have recently discovered the myriad of options available through computer software programs tend to go overboard by doing too much. Remember that less is much more effective.

Make It Easy to Read Each visual should be able to be seen clearly by the entire audience. Use type no smaller than eighteen-point or three inches high when projected.

Use Color Color is more effective than black and white for a variety of reasons. First, it has more cognitive impact. People simply remember color. As a result, a color visual is more interesting, has more impact, and makes a greater impression. With the availability of color printers and other pieces of technology, using color is easy.

Another important consideration is that audiences expect color. Even classic black-and-white films have been "colorized." Why? Because people are put off by black and white.

Keep in mind, however, that some people are color-blind. It has been estimated that 20 percent of men cannot distinguish all the colors of the spectrum, so colored objects or words appear as shades of gray, black, and white, varying only in degrees of lightness and darkness. The more distinction you can create among colors, the easier those with color blindness will be able to see.

Use It, Then Lose It Because the visual is an aid, it should be visible only when it is relevant to the point being made. When you are finished with the aid, remove it and turn off the projector. Otherwise, participants may continue to focus on the visual aid or the hum of the fan in the projector and pay little or no attention to what you are saying. People are easily distracted as it is, so do not give them anything that might divert them from your important message.

COMMONLY USED VISUAL AIDS

Although there are many visual aids from which to choose, the most widely used by trainers are the flip chart and the overhead projector. The following are some guidelines for using these effectively.

Flip-Chart Pad and Easel

The flip chart has two different applications: (1) prepared pages and (2) blank pages on which to capture information spontaneously throughout the session. Let's start with prepared pages.

Guidelines for Using Flip Charts Prepared pages are used the same way as slides or transparencies, but they tend to communicate a more casual approach or atmosphere. A major advantage of prepared pages is that you can take the time to make sure the printing is neat and legible. This is particularly important if you have a problem writing legibly. Another advantage is that valuable session time is not spent at the easel; you can show the information quickly and move on. As with other forms of visual aids, the pages double as notes for the presenter.

For blank pages used to present or capture information as you move through the session, consider these important dos and don'ts. First, if you have asked for input from participants and are capturing their responses, write down exactly what is said. Do not translate the information into your own words.

What if the person responding has a difficult time making his or her point succinctly? Some people do. There are two different approaches that can be used: (1) After listening intently to the person's response, ask the individual to summarize his or her point in a few words so that you can capture it on the flip chart or (2) if the person is not able to condense his or her point, paraphrase what you heard and ask permission to write down your interpretation of the contribution. As training guru Bob Pike says, "People don't argue with their own data." But they may argue with yours, so make sure you are respectful of their words and intent.

In full-day or half-day sessions, it is a good idea to tear off the sheets and tape them to the wall. Before doing so, however, put a brief descriptive title at the top of each sheet. To save time, cut one-inch masking tape into two- to three-inch strips before the session begins. That will enable you to post the sheets quickly.

Depending on the wall covering, you might be able to use push pins. If you are not permitted to use either tape or pins, a safe alternative is to use a magnetic dry-erase easel pad that clings to most wall surfaces and can be positioned and repositioned on the wall. The sheets are erasable and reusable as long as you use dry erase markers. Do not write on a sheet after it is posted on the wall because many markers have a tendency to bleed through! Be sure to use washable markers just in case.

If you are using blank pages to write down points as you go, you may want to prepare some pages ahead of time in light pencil so that you will not have to look at your notes. This is especially helpful for complex material. Just think how brilliant your participants will think you are that you do not have to refer to your notes.

Guidelines for Writing on Flip Charts

Whichever method you choose, the following guidelines will help you create a polished, professional image for your participants:

- Use flip charts with relatively small groups of no more than twenty-five or thirty participants.
- Print in block letters two to three inches high so that everyone in the room can see the information.
- Do not put more than about six lines of information on a page.

- Do not fill the page to the bottom. Because people are sitting, their vertical range of vision is somewhat limited.
- Do not talk to the easel while you are writing.
- Wait at least twenty to thirty seconds after you finish writing before flipping the page so that people can copy the information if they wish.
- Do not stand in front of the easel after you have finished writing. Give people an opportunity to capture the information.
- Consider using two or more easels at the front of the room to develop a continuous, uninterrupted flow of ideas or if you cannot post sheets on the wall.
- If possible, choose easel pads with perforated sheet tops for easy tearing. Use white paper, and do not use flip-chart paper with dark lines on it; it looks unprofessional.
- Use a wide, felt-tipped watercolor marker that will not bleed through the paper.
- Leave blank sheets in between, particularly if you have prepared some pages ahead of time. Unless the paper is quite opaque, the writing on the page underneath will show through.
- Be mindful of the impact of color. Use blue, green, brown, and black to add variety and interest. Save red for emphasis. Also, do not use red and green on the same page. Those who are color-blind will not be able to distinguish the two colors.
- Alternate colors by lines to make reading easier.
- Use colors systematically: one for page heading, one for primary points, another for subpoints.
- When you are not writing, put the marker down.

Overhead Projector and Transparencies

Transparencies are great for medium-sized and small audiences. They are easy to make and to use, but as with any other visual aid, they can be misused easily.

Preparing Transparencies There are several ways of creating transparencies—a method for every pocketbook.

Inexpensive. At the low end, buy a box of clear transparencies and write in colored markers right on the acetate. As a step up, purchase a box of colored transparencies made especially for either a laser printer or a photocopier. If using a laser printer, generate text from your computer, loading the transparency film into your printer. If you have a piece of printed material you would like to make into a transparency, substitute transparency film for paper in your copier. In both cases, the background will be colored, but the print will be black.

Moderate. Some people prefer colored lettering. If that is the case, several options are available. One is to purchase a colored printer for your computer and generate the document. Another is to purchase a thermal copier and different boxes of heat-sensitive thermal film of various types. A rainbow assortment allows you to create red, blue, green, or purple print on a clear background. Blue transparencies that produce yellow print on a blue background and black transparencies that give clear lettering are also available. Different colors of lettering can be created on the black background by putting different colors of transparencies behind the clear lettering.

Another interesting option is to buy special ColorBurst™ Write-On film and ColorBurst™ markers that produce a colored image on a royal-blue background. This option works much like the flip-chart pages to capture or present information as you go. It has the advantage of being somewhat unique and, therefore, captures the audience's attention.

Costly. At the upper end are professionally prepared transparencies. Many mail-order service bureaus offer custom transparencies and slides. Depending on your purpose and the number of times you intend to use the transparencies, you may choose this route. Generate your own text on your computer and send the disk to the service bureau, or ask the service bureau or a graphic designer to create the transparencies or slides for you.

Guidelines for Using Transparencies   In addition to the basic guidelines for all visual aids in terms of type size, simplicity, and use of color, the transparency presents some unique advantages as well as important considerations.

Creativity. The transparency lends itself to creativity with the use of a little imagination. In addition to the different types of film mentioned earlier, you can create an "active" transparency with a layered effect. For example, you could create a transparency with key words and then cut the film apart so you have several "mini-transparencies." Then you could create a hinge effect by laying each word on the projector as you announce or refer to it.

Framing. Professionals' transparencies are framed. Framing a transparency blocks unnecessary light, provides rigidity, makes it easier to handle, and creates a more polished appearance. Once again, there are options, depending on cost and personal preference. One way is to purchase a box of cardboard frames on which to mount the transparency with transparent tape.

Another option is to purchase an Instaframe®, a plastic frame with a glass insert. Simply place the frame on the overhead projector and put the individual transparencies on and take them off as you use them. This enables you to store your transparencies any way you choose—in a box, folder, notebook, or envelope—without purchasing more frames.

A third framing option is to purchase the 3M® Company's FlipFrame™, a transparent sleeve in which to insert the transparency. It has hinged flaps that when "flipped out" form a frame around the transparency and provide room for notes that no one else can see. FlipFrames™ are hole-punched along the left side so they can be put in a binder for better organization and protection.

Control. We have all been in sessions in which the overhead projector became an annoyance because the trainer did not control its use properly. For example, participants should never have to look at a blank screen with a blinding light. Put the transparency on the platform, then turn on the projector. Turn off the projector before you remove the transparency.

Some people believe that the process of turning the screen on and off for many transparencies is a nuisance to both the presenter and the audience. There are ways around this annoyance and inconvenience. Cut a square of heavy paper or cardboard the size of the lens aperture; attach it with masking tape in hinge-like fashion to the top of the lens casing. Instead of turning off the projector between transparencies, simply bring down the hinged cover, creating a black screen.

Similarly, lay a sheet of paper or cardboard on the platform to block the light. A remote device can be purchased from an electronics store that enables the projector to be turned on or off from several feet away. This is particularly effective when you are going to talk at some length before showing the next transparency or if you have moved into the audience and do not want to break the mood by returning to the front of the room to turn off the projector.

Another aspect of control involves the way in which you use the overhead projector. The purpose of an overhead projector is to allow you to show the visual while interacting with the participants. You can call attention to specific points on the transparency without turning your back on the group.

The group's attention can be directed in several ways by using the transparency. One way is to cover the transparency with a sheet of paper; as you make each point, uncover the word or line on the transparency. That way, the participants will read only what you want them to read and when. Remember that this technique annoys many people. Another way is to use a pointer or pen to direct participants' attention to key words on the transparency. Any standard or retractable pointer will do, but you might want to make things more interesting by purchasing specialty pointers, such as the one sold by Creative Training Techniques or that are available in novelty stores.

Still another method of calling attention to specific information on the transparency is to use a transparency marker to underline or circle key points as you go. A word of advice: absolutely never point at the screen itself! Your arm will create a shadow on the screen, which is not only distracting, but also obstructs the full view of the screen. Another reason for not pointing to the screen is that it causes you to turn away from the group, taking away the advantage of maintaining direct contact with the group. The final reason for not pointing to the screen is to avoid damaging the screen with the pointer.

The last piece of advice about using an overhead projector is to dim the lights near the screen to create a sharp contrast and make it easier for the audience to see the visual.

Videos and Video Clips

Video clips can be used in much the same way as demonstrations or scripted role plays. As with other media and methods, there are several options. Use a small portion from a movie or television show to illustrate a point. This is very effective, but be sure to obtain written permission. Copyright laws are not to be taken lightly. However, there are libraries of copyright-free video clips for use in presentations. Also, news clips and other events captured on film are often in the public domain.

One way around the cost and inconvenience of dealing with copyrighted material is to create your own video clips. The quality largely depends on the amount of money you are willing or able to spend. Use a video camera or hire a professional videographer to help produce the video, keeping in mind that the greatest expense is associated with the editing process.

You could write your own script and use your friends, colleagues, or acting students from a local college or university to illustrate the points, skills, or concepts through short vignettes. It is a great opportunity for aspiring or non-professional actors to obtain both experience and exposure.

Computer-Based Media

Computer-generated slides take the place of transparencies and 35 mm slides. The equipment requirements include a computer and an LCD panel with an overhead projector or an LCD projector. Computer capabilities enable you to create professional and polished shows with animation, sound, special effects, and even video enhancements. The flexibility of the media enables you to modify information on a moment's notice to reflect late-breaking developments or audience input. On the down side, this equipment is expensive and, because the technology is changing so rapidly, it becomes outdated fairly quickly. Unfortunately, trainers with this capability often rely too heavily on using this medium and deliver passive rather than active training.

Figure 9.1 provides a summary of the advantages and disadvantages of various visual aids covered in this Module.

FIGURE 9.1. Using Visual Aids

Aid	Advantages	Disadvantages	When to Use
Chalkboards	• Spontaneous • Easy to use • Inexpensive • Erasable • Attention grabber • Breaks lecture monotony	• Slow • Temporary • Poor readability • Limited to chalk • Back turned to audience • Associated with school days • Messy	• Small, informal meetings • Spontaneous idea development • Brainstorming sessions
Flip Charts	• Spontaneous • Advance preparation • Better contrast • Permanent • Easy to use • Portable • Allows ideas to be presented in sequence • Inexpensive • Range of colors available • Dependable	• Bulky • Limited to writing • No flexibility in size or sequence • Expensive if prepared • Tendency to write small to put all ideas on one page • Paper tears easily	• Small groups • Lectures with spontaneous highlighting • Brainstorming • Lists, procedural steps
35 mm Slides	• High quality • Photographic detail • Very portable • Easy to operate • Can accommodate any size group • Voice can be integrated • Trainer can use remote and move around	• Dark room • Usually expensive • Can appear "canned" • Slides become focal point, not speaker • Does not show motion • Long sequences encourage mental absenteeism	• Repetitive programs for which photographic detail and professional look are important • Training programs or product displays with sound and music added

FIGURE 9.1. *Continued*

Aid	Advantages	Disadvantages	When to Use
Overhead Projector	• Fast, simple preparation • Lights on • Speaker faces audience • Any size group • Spontaneous or advance preparation • Very flexible • Optional quality • Inexpensive • Exact illustrations can be portrayed • Easily updated	• Projector can block view • Less portable than slides • May make too "busy" because of ease of preparation • Tendency to overuse • Focus sometimes difficult to control	• Financial and technical presentations • Sales presentations • Seminars, workshops in which speaker wants to maintain rapport
Videos	• Professional • Good discussion generator • Immediate feedback • Any size group • Effective for showing how *not* to act • Most effective for learner-centered training • Both sight and hearing are utilized • "Expert" on tape reinforces message	• Dark room • Expensive • May be substitute for lesson or presentation	• Supplement to a training program • Visual feedback of trainee performance • Create mood or feeling as prelude to speaker's presentation

◆   ◆   ◆

Module Ten

Working with Groups

LEARNING OUTCOMES

In this module, you will learn

- To stimulate discussion among participants
- To master the art of asking and answering questions
- To deal with difficult people and situations

THE TRAINER AS FACILITATOR

Standing in front of a group and presenting information is one thing; facilitating discussion and interaction is another. Each requires a different set of skills. If you accept the changing role of the trainer—from "teacher" to "facilitator"—then you will have to understand and develop facilitation skills.

Any time you work *with* a group in a participant-centered environment instead of talking *at* that group, you are facilitating the learning process. Facilitation skills are particularly critical for processing activities, as discussed in Module Eight.

The most important thing to remember about your responsibilities as a trainer is that you are a *role model*. How you conduct yourself verbally and nonverbally determines how participants conduct themselves.

WAYS TO ENCOURAGE PARTICIPATION

Your behavior throughout the session sends a message that either encourages or discourages participation. Sometimes these messages are pretty straightfor-

Note: Material in this module is taken from Lawson, K. (1998). *Involving your audience: Make it active.* Needham Heights, MA: Allyn and Bacon.

ward; sometimes they are much more subtle. Not only are subtle messages communicated without our awareness, but their impact can be quite powerful.

Nonverbal Communication

What you do often speaks more loudly than what you say. Use the power of these nonverbal communication techniques to encourage participation:

- *Eye Contact*. Be attentive to making eye contact with all participants.
- *Head Nodding*. Nod your head to show understanding and to encourage participants to continue.
- *Posture*. Avoid defensive postures such as folded arms.
- *Body Movement*. Avoid distracting movements such as too much walking or pacing. Move toward people to draw them into the discussion.
- *Smile*. Concentrate on smiling with both mouth and eyes to encourage and relax the group.

Verbal Communication

What you say and how you say it can either shut down or encourage participation. Be mindful of the difference between intent and perception. Frequently conduct your own reality check by asking yourself: "What is my intent, and how am I being perceived?" Practice using the following techniques to create an exciting and positive learning environment.

Praise or Encourage Use simple, but powerful, words of encouragement to prod the participant to continue:

- "I'm glad you brought that up."
- "Tell me more."
- "Okay, let's build on that."
- "Good point. Who else has an idea?"
- "I would like to hear your thoughts about. . . ."

Accept or Use Ideas Clarify, build on, and further develop ideas suggested by another participant:

- "To piggyback on your point, Juan, . . ."
- As Salina mentioned earlier, . . ."

Accept Feelings   Use statements that communicate acceptance and clarification of feelings:

- "I sense that you are upset by what I just said."
- "You seem to feel very strongly about this issue."
- "I know it's hard to maintain a positive outlook when you are at risk of being a downsizing casualty."
- "I can imagine that you feel. . . ."

THE ART OF QUESTIONING

The art of asking questions is central to your success as a facilitator of adult learning. The key is to ask questions that stimulate discussion and interaction, rather than questions that elicit simple factual responses reminiscent of grade school. To stimulate discussion, be sure your questions are open-ended.

People often think they are asking open-ended questions when they are not. An open-ended question is one that begins with *who, what, where, when, why,* or *how.* Questions that begin with these words will elicit a more detailed and meaningful response from participants. Closed-ended questions, on the other hand, are questions that someone could answer with a simple "yes" or "no" and certainly do not encourage participation. To make it easy, try to ask questions that begin with *how* or *what.* If you are in the habit of asking these kinds of questions, your group discussions and processing segments will be very effective.

Avoid using questions that begin with *why. Why* questions tend to put people on the defensive. They may feel that they have to explain and justify their responses.

Different types of questions obtain different results. Practice using questions that match your desired outcome. For example, if you want to start the discussion, ask a general question of the entire group. For example, in a customer-service program, you might ask, "How do you think your organization is doing in terms of delivering quality service?" This type of question prompts people to express an opinion. Because there are likely to be a variety of opinions offered, interest is generated in the topic and the discussion is underway. You may next want to uncover the reasons behind the opinions just expressed, so ask a specific question such as, "What are some examples of situations that lead you to believe that your organization's level of customer service [is outstanding, needs improvement]?"

After you have asked the question, be quiet. Trainers have a tendency to ask a question, and when no one responds immediately, they answer the question themselves. Silence, of course, is uncomfortable, and you may feel that you have to speak up to fill the void. Let silence happen. Learn to ask the question and then be silent for ten or twelve seconds to give people time to think of their responses. If you keep answering your own questions, there is no reason for participants to offer their ideas.

RESPONDING TO QUESTIONS

In a lively, risk-free, and dynamic environment, participants will be stimulated to ask questions as well as answer them. Although this is certainly what you want to happen, this type of participant interaction can be quite challenging.

Reasons People Ask Questions

Before addressing some of the dos and don'ts of fielding questions from the group, let's look at the reasons people want the opportunity to ask questions. Understanding their motivation will help you better prepare for both the expected and unexpected.

To Obtain Information or to Clarify No matter how clear you were in delivering a message, the participants will not all process and understand the information in the same way or at the same time. Some will want and need additional information to help them understand points more clearly or to satisfy their desire for more detail. They may want further assurance that you know what you are talking about.

Something you said earlier may have ignited a spark of curiosity or may provoke an interest in finding out more about a topic. In the latter case, they will ask questions about other resources and will expect you to point them in the right direction. Even if you have provided a bibliography or recommended reading list, some will want you to recommend or identify sources for specific interests and pursuits.

To Impress Others Every group has one or more people who like to ask questions as an opportunity to be noticed either by peers or someone at a higher level. Being in the spotlight may satisfy some people's ego needs. For others, it affords the chance to demonstrate qualities such as assertiveness and risk taking or to showcase their knowledge of the subject as a means to career advancement.

To "Get" the Trainer For various reasons, some participants will not like the trainer or what he or she has to say. They take every opportunity to make the trainer look bad or see him or her squirm purely for their own amusement. They may see this as a chance to "get even" or undermine a trainer's credibility.

To Help the Trainer At the other end of the scale are participants who really like the trainer and want to help him or her look good. If they agree with the trainer's position on a particular topic, they will want to help increase the persuasive impact even more.

To Keep from Going Back to Work Some people may ask questions as a way to prolong the session, thus avoid returning to work, particularly if the session is due to be over near the end of the day. They may reason that the more questions they ask and the more time they can take up, there will not be enough time to accomplish anything back on the job anyway and they will be dismissed early.

Guidelines for Handling Questions

To master the art of responding to questions, consider the following guidelines.

Set Ground Rules in the Beginning At the beginning of the session, tell the participants how questions will be handled: throughout the session; at intervals; or at the end. If you encourage people to ask questions as they think of them, you may need to limit the number of questions or the time spent addressing them in order to stay on schedule. The important thing is to communicate clearly when you will and will not take questions. If you plan to wait until the end of a section to take questions, suggest that they write their questions down so they do not forget them.

Repeat the Question Sometimes a trainer's answer to a question is totally off the mark, probably as a result of not taking the time to clarify and confirm what he or she thought the participant actually asked. Sometimes, the person asking the question is not very articulate and may have a difficult time stating the question concisely and succinctly.

Repeat or paraphrase the question before answering it. Repeating the question accomplishes three things:

- It ensures that the rest of the group has heard the question.
- It ensures that you have heard the question correctly.
- It buys a little time to organize your thoughts before answering.

To ensure that the question is the same as intended, paraphrase the question by saying, "If I heard you correctly, your question is. . . . Is that right?" If the question is long, ask if you may reword it, then restate it concisely and check to see that you indeed captured the essence of the question. Do not, however, paraphrase by using any of these phrases:

- "What you mean is. . . ."
- "What you're saying is. . . ."
- "What you're trying to say is. . . ."

These phrases are insulting and condescending. The subtle message is: "You're obviously not articulate in expressing yourself, so let me help you out."

Use Eye Contact Look at the person who asked the question while you are paraphrasing to make sure you understood the question. When you deliver your response, direct it to the entire group, not just the person who asked the question.

Choose Words Carefully Choose words carefully and think about the impact they may have on individual participants. Avoid using words such as "obviously." This implies that the person asking the question should already know the answer. Along the same line, phrases such as "You have to understand" come across as ordering and directing. "You should" sounds like preaching or moralizing.

Respect the Group Never belittle or embarrass a participant. This means that sometimes you have to exercise a little patience, particularly when someone asks a question that you have already addressed in the session. Absolutely never say, "As I already mentioned." Instead, answer the question by carefully rewording your point so that you are not repeating the remark exactly as you said it earlier.

Responding to Individual Concerns Sometimes a participant will ask a question that is extremely narrowly focused and pertains only to himself or herself. If that happens, give a brief response and then suggest that the two of you talk about it after the session. Use this same strategy with those who ask questions unrelated to the topic. Always indicate your openness and willingness to talk further one-on-one. Above all else, project compassion and concern.

Cover All Parts of the Room Trainers sometimes have a tendency to look only to the right or to the left and, as a result, entertain questions from only one side of the room. Although the habit is unintentional, people on the side being ignored will become anxious and annoyed. Similarly, some trainers will acknowledge participants who are in the front because it is easy both to see and to hear them. Make a concerted effort to take questions from all parts of the audience.

Do Not Bluff Sometimes people may ask questions that you cannot answer. Be honest. Do not be afraid to say, "I don't know." However, do not leave it at that. Offer to check further and get back to them by phone or mail or at a later session or tell them where they can find the additional information themselves.

Things Not to Say In an effort to be supportive and encouraging, trainers will often respond to a participant by saying, "That's a good question." The danger here is that you may come across as patronizing or insincere. Also, others who do not receive the same feedback or reinforcement may feel their questions were not as "good." Instead, comment by saying, "That's an interesting question" or "That's an intriguing question." Similarly, a response such as "I'm glad you asked that question" may be understood by others to mean that you are not glad that they asked a question.

After you have responded, do not say, "Does that answer your question?" What happens if the participant responds that you did not answer the question? Worse still, the participant may not have had his or her question answered but does not want to embarrass you or himself/herself and just lets it go. By asking if you answered the question, you give up some control and suggest a lack of confidence in your answer. A better response is, "What other questions do you have?" or "Would you like me to go into more detail?"

This is a much more gracious and face-saving approach for both the trainer and the participant. It also gives the participant an opportunity to clarify his or her question or probe a little further, if necessary, so that he or she is satisfied.

SCALING THE WALL OF RESISTANCE

It is quite probable that you will experience some resistance from individuals, or even entire groups. Unless you can overcome that resistance, you will have a very difficult time achieving your learning objectives. The first step in scaling the wall of resistance is to recognize it so that you can deal with it before it undermines the learning process.

Recognizing Resistance

Resistance among participants takes many forms. Some people bring work to the session and busy themselves with that rather than paying attention. Others might bring in a newspaper and start reading it. Some ask antagonistic questions, while others will not open their mouths or even crack a smile.

Because symptoms of resistance are so varied, be observant and look for behaviors that may indicate a potential problem. Pay particular attention to facial expressions and other nonverbal communication. If participants look angry, confused, or bored, be ready to acknowledge it and deal with it.

Causes of Resistance

In order to deal with resistance and prevent dysfunctional behavior, you must first understand it. In many cases, you will have to address the underlying psychological climate. Some possible reasons for resistance are covered below.

Do Not Want to Be There Sometimes participants just do not want to be there. Often people resent attending a session. Perhaps they feel they are being punished, or they may feel overwhelmed by their work load and do not believe they can afford to take time away from the job.

CASE OF RESISTANCE TO TRAINING

I was asked to conduct a session on performance appraisal for first-line supervisors in a manufacturing setting. During an assessment meeting with the vice president of operations, I sensed that there might be some resistance to the training, so I discussed the importance of explaining to the supervisors why the company was investing time and money in this program and how they could benefit from attending. The vice president agreed to communicate that message. The morning of the session, I met briefly with the vice president, who assured me that he had prepared the participants as I had suggested. Breathing a sigh of relief, I walked into the room only to be confronted by nineteen frowning men with their arms folded, seated in a horseshoe configuration. Although the situation did not look good, I was confident that I could bring them around. I started with an appropriate icebreaker and opening activities. The supervisors absolutely refused to participate. After several failed attempts to break through the stone wall of resistance, I stopped and said, "Guys, it's clear to me that something's going on here, and I think we need to talk about it. Let me ask you a question. Why do you think the company is offering this session?" With that, the flood gates opened, and I was bombarded with comments such as "Beats the [expletive] out of me" and "I guess we must be doing a pretty [expletive] job and now we're being punished." I spent the next forty-five minutes just talking with the group and helping them see how this session could help them do their jobs better. Clearly, the vice president had not done his job.

Do Not Know Why They Are There Believe it or not, some people walk into a session and have no idea why they were asked to attend. Sometimes, they do not even know what the topic is.

CASE OF NOT KNOWING WHY

I had been engaged to do a two-hour session on communication for line employees at a packaging plant. As I frequently do, I asked the participants why they were there and what they hoped to learn. I was surprised to find that they thought they were attending a safety-training session. I used the situation as an opportunity to stress the importance of communication in the workplace. I even managed to tie communication to safety issues and how good communication could prevent accidents and safety violations. Because I was able to adjust my design on the spot to meet the needs of my participants, the session was a success.

Personal Issues Session participants are human beings, and human beings have personal lives and problems that sometimes get in the way of learning new things. Some may simply not feel well. Others may be preoccupied with a personal problem.

CASE OF PERSONAL ISSUES

I was delivering a three-day management-development program when a woman in her late forties or early fifties told me during a break that her husband of twenty-five years had just left her for a much younger woman. It was obvious from her demeanor and tone of voice that she was miserable, which was reflected in her behavior during the session. She was argumentative and confrontational, challenging and contradicting everything I said and being downright difficult and unpleasant. Every time I said something, she attacked it. I tried every technique I knew, but nothing worked. I decided to take our mid-morning break early and went into a private office to calm down and regain my composure. When we reconvened, she had toned down. One of the participants later told me that several of her fellow participants had talked to the woman during break and told her that her behavior was inappropriate. In situations like this one, quite often others in the group will deal directly with the difficult person.

Attitude Toward Boss or Organization If a participant has negative feelings about the organization or his or her manager, the individual will bring that negativity into the session. The resentment is transferred to the trainer. Whether you are internal or external, the "boss" or the organization hired you. You are guilty by association and automatically are viewed as "one of them." This is further amplified when the participants do not see a real commitment to training on the part of the organization. Participants will often remark, "My boss should be attending this training, too."

Sessions dealing with change present a particular problem. For many, the session only serves to magnify the change or changes they are experiencing, and, in many cases, the participants are not happy about these changes.

CASE OF PROBLEMS WITH A BOSS

At the beginning of a program on managing change and stress, I asked participants to share the most difficult or troublesome changes they were currently experiencing. One man was quite emotional when he related that he was moving his office from the suburbs to the city. As the day progressed, we learned that he had been with the company thirty years, enjoyed six weeks' vacation, and earned a very comfortable salary. In our discussion about values, he was quite clear that money, material possessions, and vacation time were very important to him.

At one point in the program, I emphasized that in dealing with change, we all have choices, and those choices are based on many things, including our values, personality types, family situations, and so forth. As I finished my statement about having choices, the man started yelling at me, "You don't understand! I don't have a choice in moving my office! I'm sick of you high-priced consultants coming in here and telling us what we should do. You have no idea what you're talking about." He continued his tirade, and I sat down and allowed him to run out of steam. After he was finished, I told him that I could see his point and that I was sorry this change was causing him such distress.

Very likely his feeling of powerlessness and the resulting anger and frustration had been smoldering for some time. The discussion triggered an intense emotional response that was really directed toward the company. Although he may have seen me as a representative of the "enemy," I was not in a position of power and, therefore, was a safe target on which to unleash his pent-up hostility.

Attitude Toward Topic Not every participant will be happy with the topic, particularly if his or her attendance has been mandated. This is particularly true when presenting controversial topics such as diversity or sexual harassment. Some participants are quite open and candid about their perception that the topic is being "shoved down their throats."

CASE OF DISLIKE OF TOPIC

In a session I conducted on sexual harassment for a group of bank managers, one man expressed his disapproval of the entire subject by saying, "If women don't like the way they're treated, let them go work elsewhere." I pointed out to him that although he was certainly entitled to his personal feelings, in his role as a manager, he had a responsibility to support his organization's policy as well as the law of the land.

Pushed Out of Their Comfort Zones Particularly in human relations training, participants are challenged to look at themselves, situations, and beliefs a different way. Managers who have been using a traditional and autocratic style of managing may be required to learn new approaches and philosophies that are more democratic and participatory. People who have been working on their own as individual contributors may be expected to learn how to work in a team environment. New organizational expectations require employees to learn new skills and assume new roles. For example, a bank customer-service representative may be expected to sell banking services. Many people are uncomfortable and unsure of themselves in new roles, and that insecurity creates a barrier to learning. As a trainer, you not only must help them to develop new skills but also to see how they might personally benefit from new roles and responsibilities.

Literacy Problems If people have a difficult time reading, they may be resistant to attending a session that requires them to do anything that involves reading, such as case studies, written exercises, and assessment instruments. Trainers must be observant of behavior that suggests a literacy problem and make every effort to work with people so that they can succeed.

Language Problems For those who are not fluent in the language in which the session is being delivered, the experience can be frustrating and unpleasant. Because of their frustration and difficulty in understanding what the trainer is saying, they may act out their frustration by being difficult and uncooperative, either intentionally or unintentionally. As the workplace becomes more diverse, this issue will become an even greater challenge for trainers.

Past Experiences Some participants may have had unpleasant learning experiences either in school or as adults attending other work-sponsored programs. Often they come to the session expecting it to be much of the same, and they are braced to expect the worst. Sometimes this comes out at the end of a session.

CASE OF COMPARING PAST EXPERIENCES

Depending on the group, and particularly if I sense some resistance early on, I ask the group during the feedback portion of the session: "Was this program different from what you expected?" The answer is always "yes." When I probe further, participants usually tell me that they expected it to be dull and boring. Some will say that they thought I would just lecture or talk "at" them. They will often add that my approach was a pleasant surprise and made the experience both meaningful and enjoyable.

Effects of Resistance

Now that we have looked at the causes of participant resistance, let's take a look at the effects. Left unchecked, resistance can divide the group into factions, polarizing them against you or one another. These negative behaviors interfere with learning. No one can learn in an environment dominated by disruptive behavior. Additionally, undesirable behaviors cause emotional stress and anxiety for the trainer as well as for those who are witnessing the shenanigans.

PROBLEM SITUATIONS

No matter how well you have planned and prepared for a workshop or seminar, more often than not, something unexpected will happen. Sometimes what started out as a terrific session turns into your worst nightmare. Some human behavior, attitudes, or reactions are predictable. It is your job as a trainer to anticipate these behaviors, to prevent them if you can, and, if not, to deal with them effectively.

Prevention Strategies

Often, problems in a training session can be avoided through proper planning, preparation, anticipation, and communication.

Planning When designing a training session, consider the various learning styles and perceptual modalities discussed in Module Two. Be sure to use interactive techniques and do not be afraid to be creative, even outrageous. Also use a variety of methods and media to appeal to various styles.

Planning also involves having a back-up plan for equipment problems, materials that do not arrive, schedule changes, and activities that might not work with a particular group of participants.

Preparation The importance of finding out as much as possible about participants through the use of questionnaires and surveys, interviews, and discussions with their managers has already been covered. It is also a good idea to send something to the participants ahead of time: an interesting, attention-getting flyer, a short article to read, or anything that will pique their interest and prepare them for the session. You might assign readings or other prework.

Anticipation For full-day or half-day sessions, make sure to request (or bring) the accoutrements that help create a professional environment. These include tent cards, pads and pencils, water, quality participant materials, and dishes with wrapped candies. This communicates a message to the participants: This session is important. A professional touch will help set the tone and make it more difficult for people to act up. For sessions of three hours or more, make sure there are refreshments available during breaks. Not only is this reflective of a professional touch, but it shows consideration for the participants.

CASE OF MEETING NEEDS

During an all-day session for a trade association, the meeting planner and I learned a valuable lesson about the importance of meeting participants' basic needs. The meeting planner had arranged for coffee and tea to be available when participants arrived for the workshop. The participants, however, noted on their evaluation sheets the conspicuous absence of doughnuts, muffins, or bagels; their disappointment impacted their overall rating of the session.

Also keep in mind that many people today forgo the traditional coffee and tea in favor of soft drinks, juices, and bottled water. Health-conscious and calorie-conscious participants also prefer fresh fruit to pastries.

Communication   Sometimes, no matter how well you plan, prepare, and even anticipate, you may be faced with a particularly difficult group. Sometimes groups as a whole behave as a single entity. The key to dealing with these situations is to be able to size up the audience and quickly adapt your style accordingly.

If you sense that you have a difficult or even hostile group, consider addressing the issue up front. Ask questions such as, "What concerns do you have about today's session?" or "Why do you think the company is offering this program?" This brings issues out on the table so that you can address them. As participants are expressing their issues and feelings, capture the information on the flip chart. Remain objective, nonjudgmental, and empathetic. Facilitate a discussion or an activity that forces the group to come up with solutions or recommendations. Do not take responsibility for solving the problem yourself.

If a group is particularly disruptive or, at the other extreme, shuts down completely and will not participate, use the "divide-and-conquer" technique. Break the group into pairs or subgroups and give each a specific assignment. Pose questions similar to the ones in the previous paragraph or have them come up with a list of suggestions related to the topic.

Another effective tool is the "parking lot." Post a flip chart with the words "Parking Lot" at the top. Give participants Post-it™ Notes and explain that if issues come up unrelated to the topic, to jot them on the Post-it™ Notes and put them in the "parking lot." This technique allows the participants to acknowledge their issues and concerns and get them out of the way. Say, "Your point is well taken, although it's not relevant to what we're talking about now. Write it down and put it in the 'parking lot,' and we'll be sure to address it before the end of the session."

Personal Attacks

Personal attacks may be triggered by something you say that strikes a nerve with a participant, or the attacks could come from a "professional heckler" who just enjoys the challenge of putting you on the spot and making you squirm.

Far less annoying, but offering a different challenge, is the person who begins attacking you because he or she disagrees with something you said.

CASE OF PERSONAL ATTACK

For example, I was conducting an all-day workshop for a group of managers, talking about the importance of managers communicating clearly their standards of performance and expectations to their employees. I also emphasized the need to include guidelines or parameters as part of those expectations.

I decided to use a personal parenting example to illustrate my point. I had learned through earlier questioning that 95 percent of the audience members were parents. I related an incident involving my fourteen-year-old stepson many years earlier. I created the appropriate backdrop for the story by explaining that fourteen-year-olds go through a "black period" during which everything they wear is black. So when my stepson wanted to redecorate his room, I thought it would be prudent to tell him that he could decorate his room any way he wanted except for two things: he could not paint his walls black, and he could not put up posters of nude women. The audience laughed, as always when I tell that story.

Before I could go on to draw a parallel between parents setting parameters and managers doing the same, I was interrupted by a man yelling at me from the back of the room: "How could you do such a thing? That was your son's room, and you have no right telling him what he can and cannot do with his own space!" As he continued his ranting, I interrupted by saying, "I can certainly understand your point of view. However, we're not here to debate parenting philosophy. I was making a point that, just as parents have the right to set standards and expectations for their children, managers have the right to set standards and expectations for their employees. And in both cases, one person's standards may be quite different from another's. The important thing is that you clearly communicate them and hold people accountable."

Keep Your Cool When faced with the unexpected, the most important thing to remember is to maintain your composure. Remain calm and in control. Several techniques will help in these situations:

- *Lower the Pitch of Your Voice.* When we are nervous or upset, the pitch or our voices tends to go higher, particularly for women.
- *Breathe Deeply.* Shallow breathing is a sign of nervousness and will affect the quality of the voice.
- *Control Your Speed.* Many people have a tendency to speak faster when they are under stress, so concentrate on maintaining a moderate rate when responding.
- *Control Your Volume.* Although you want to project your voice, do not shout. Maintain a reasonable volume level, loud enough to make sure you are heard, but not so loud that you sound angry or out of control.
- *Attend to Nonverbals.* Avoid nervous gestures such as fiddling with clothes, jewelry, paper clips, or pointer. Those are a dead giveaway that you are losing control. Also, be careful not to appear in a counterattack mode. If you gesture, keep your palms open and do not point.

Handle Challenges with Grace and Professionalism Accept the fact that you are not always correct. If someone points out an error, thank the individual. Do not be defensive. Sometimes an individual may challenge you by offering a different opinion or point of view. When that happens, acknowledge the difference of opinion and thank the person for offering a different point of view. Do not, however, be drawn into an argument or a debate.

People automatically ask questions that start with "why." Quite naturally, you may have a tendency to react defensively. To avoid delivering a defensive-sounding response, reframe the "why" into a "how" or "what" question when you restate it. For example, if someone poses the following question, "Why did you . . . ?, reframe it by saying, "If I understand you correctly, you're asking me *how* I. . . ." Or "As I understand it, you want to know *what* I. . . ." When responding to these challenging questions, begin with "In my experience . . ." or present facts or quote experts as appropriate.

Participant Behavior

More often than not, the group as a whole is not a problem, but there may be a few difficult people in the session. Here are some coping strategies for dealing with specific types.

Talkative The talkative participant has something to say about everything. This person always volunteers to be a group leader, answer questions, or offer suggestions. He or she seems to want to be the center of attention. To deal with the talkative type, say something like, "I appreciate your contribution, but let's hear from some other people." Suggest further discussion at break or lunch by saying, "In order to stay on schedule and on track, let's discuss this further during the break or after the session."

Clueless This person seems to have no idea what is going on. He or she totally misunderstands the question or the topic being discussed. As a result, this person's answers or remarks do not even remotely relate to the subject under discussion. For this person, say, "Something I said must have led you off track. What I was trying to say is. . . ."

Rambling This person goes on and on about nothing. He or she digresses frequently and uses examples and analogies that do not relate to the topic being discussed. This person is different from the "clueless" individual in that the rambler knows what is going on but prefers to follow his or her own agenda. To put this person back on track, try asking, "I don't understand. How does this relate to what we're talking about?" This is a good opportunity to use the "parking lot."

Belligerent The belligerent person is openly hostile, challenging and arguing every point. This person questions the trainer's knowledge and credibility and may even accuse the trainer of being "out of touch" with the real world. Do not engage in any verbal sparring. Say to this person, "I understand and appreciate your point of view. What do some of the rest of you think?" By turning to the rest of the group, you take yourself off the hook and give others an opportunity to exert some peer pressure to change this person's behavior. You might also offer to discuss the issue further during break.

Stubborn This individual refuses to see anyone else's point of view and is particularly difficult to deal with in a group environment. His or her refusal to give in on a point will thwart group decision-making or consensus-seeking activities. Sometimes you can take the direct approach and say, "I appreciate your position (or point of view), but for the sake of the activity (discussion, etc.), I'm going to insist that we move on. I'll be happy to discuss this with you later."

Silent Every group has one or more silent types who seem attentive and alert but will not volunteer comments or answer questions. He or she may be naturally shy or uncomfortable speaking up in a group and seems content just to listen.

You might wonder, "So what's wrong with that?" The problem is that often these quiet people have some wonderful comments and contributions to make, and if we do not make an effort to involve them, their ideas never surface and the group misses the opportunity to learn from another of its members. The participant himself or herself misses an opportunity to be heard and receive validation. Try prompting the reluctant or shy participant by saying, "[Person's name], I know you have some experience in this area. It would be helpful if you would share your thoughts with the group." Another approach is to break the group into pairs or trios. The shy person is much more likely to participate in these smaller groups.

Know-It-All The know-it-all often tries to upstage or overshadow the trainer. Often viewing himself or herself as an authority on every subject, this person assumes a superior role with both the group and the trainer. This person relishes the opportunity to flaunt his or her knowledge, often using big words, quoting facts and figures, and dropping names. Although it may be difficult, do not let your annoyance show. Acknowledge his or her contribution by saying, "That's one point of view. However, there are other ways of looking at it." Depending on the situation, ask other participants for their opinions or move on.

Class Clown The class clown is relatively harmless unless you allow him or her to get out of control. This person makes a joke out of everything and goes out of his or her way to get attention, often at the expense of others. Do not give in to this person's attempt to control the situation. Simply say, "We all enjoy a little levity. But right now, let's get serious and concentrate on the topic at hand."

Negative This individual complains about the organization, his or her boss, co-workers, you name it. In addition to the negative verbal remarks, he or she displays negative nonverbal behavior such as frowning or assuming a defensive posture. Often this person is a chronic complainer who has nothing positive to contribute. Say something like, "I understand your point. What suggestions do you have to change the situation?" Or you might say, "For the sake of discussion, what might be some arguments for the opposite point of view?"

Indifferent It is pretty clear to everyone that this person does not want to be there. He or she makes no attempt to participate or contribute. Because he or she has been forced to attend, not only will this person show no interest, but he or she may even resort to engaging in activities separate from the group. Use a tactic similar to the one you might use with the silent type: "I know you have some experience in this area. Please tell us about it."

Personality Clashes Some people in a group may not get along. They may engage in verbal battles, either directly or indirectly, often with remarks becoming very personal and hurtful. When a situation like this occurs, it is important to address it early by invoking ground rules or saying, "I suggest that we keep personalities out of the discussion. Let's get back to the topic at hand."

Side Conversations Side conversations are a frequent and annoying occurrence. Far too often, two or more members of the group engage in their own conversation while a fellow participant or the trainer is talking. More than one strategy may be needed to bring them back. Sometimes just walking over to the individuals will cause them to stop their conversation. If that does not work, try saying, "[Persons' names], we were just talking about. . . . What are your thoughts?"

General Guidelines

When dealing with any of these situations, keep in mind four important goals:

- *Stop the dysfunctional behavior.* Your first objective is to stop the disruptive behavior.
- *Keep the individual(s) engaged.* Your second objective is to prevent the person from "shutting down" and not participating at all.
- *Keep the rest of the group involved.* Your third objective is to prevent others in the group from shutting down. Keep in mind that others will judge you by the way you handle these difficult situations.
- *Respect the individual.* Your fourth objective, and perhaps the most important, is to respect the individual and help maintain his or her dignity. Do not embarrass or belittle the person.

After you have addressed a behavior or responded to a hostile participant, look toward another person or section of the room. Continued eye contact will only encourage the participant and may result in a continued debate or argument. Remember that you can never win an argument with a participant. Even if the group is annoyed with their fellow participant's behavior, if you attack that person, the others may turn against you. After all, he or she is one of them.

When participants demonstrate intense negative emotions, it is important to acknowledge those feelings and emotions with a statement such as, "I can tell you feel strongly about this" or "I'm sorry you feel that way." Be careful not to make judgmental statements such as, "You're being negative" or "You're not listening."

Learning to Live with It

One of the biggest challenges a trainer faces is to accept the fact that some people and some situations are beyond his or her control. When, despite all your efforts, the session still does not go according to plan, assess the situation as objectively as possible. Ask yourself what you could have done differently. If you conclude that you did everything you could to prevent or handle the situation, then do not fret about it. Accept the fact that people bring a lot of "baggage" to your sessions that you have no way of knowing about or controlling. On the other hand, if you think you could have handled the situation better, then learn from your mistakes and move on.

◆ ◆ ◆

Module Eleven

Creativity in the Workshop

LEARNING OUTCOMES

In this module, you will learn

- Creative ways to form subgroups
- Creative approaches to motivate and energize the group
- Ways to incorporate games into the instructional design
- How to create and maintain structure for small-group assignments
- How to use games to increase learning and improve retention
- How to adapt games to specific content and learning objectives
- To design closing activities that reinforce learning

CREATIVITY WITH SMALL GROUPS

The use of small groups is a very effective learning technique and the cornerstone of cooperative learning. Sometimes, however, when you announce that you are going to break into subgroups, you might hear, "Oh, no! Not again!" To maintain a high level of interest and enthusiasm throughout the session, draw on your creative muse, even when dealing with small groups.

Grouping Techniques

Many learning activities require you to break a large group into subgroups. The most frequently used method of creating subgroups is to ask participants to count off by however many groups you want to create. However, this method is boring and people often forget their numbers or where they are supposed to relocate. Instead of the old "ho-hum" approach, let's look at some other more creative ways to create small groups.

- *Puzzles.* Make or buy six-piece jigsaw puzzles and give each person a puzzle piece. To form subgroups, the participants have to find those who have pieces to the same puzzle.
- *Candy.* Different flavors of wrapped candy can be distributed to participants just before breaking them into groups. (Be sure to tell them not to eat the candy just yet.) Ask the peppermints to go to one spot; butterscotch kisses, another; Hershey's Kisses®, still another.
- *Participant Materials.* Give participants pens or folders of different colors to indicate their groups.
- *Grouping Cards.* Another way to move people quickly and efficiently into different configurations throughout the day is to create grouping cards. Each person receives a 3" x 5" card on which is a colored dot, a number, and a colorful sticker. The numbers, dots, and stickers are placed on the cards so that they will form random groups of varying sizes, depending on the purpose of the activity and required subgroup size. For example, say there are twelve people in a workshop and you will need to create four groups of three (red, blue, green, yellow dots), three groups of four (animal stickers: lions, giraffes, zebras), or two groups of six (numbers 1 and 2). When you are ready to put people into subgroups, tell them how to group and where.
- *Finding Famous Fictional Friends and Families.* Another excellent way to group people is called "Finding Famous Fictional Friends and Families." First, depending on the number of groups you will need, create groups of four or five fictional characters in the same "family" such as Robin Hood, Maid Marian, Friar Tuck, Little John, Sheriff of Nottingham; Tin Man, Cowardly Lion, Dorothy, Scarecrow, Toto; Peter Pan, Captain Hook, Wendy, Tinkerbell, Crocodile; Hawkeye, Hot Lips, Trapper John, Radar, Klinger. Put the names of each character on a separate index card (one card per person in the workshop), shuffle the cards, and give each participant a card. Next ask the participants to find the other members of their "families." Suggest to participants that if they do not recognize the name of the character they drew, to ask their fellow participants for help.

When the subgroups have been formed, ask them to discuss a particular topic or come up with a list related to the topic. For example, for a customer-service program, ask the groups to share the best or the worst experiences they ever had as customers. In a program on managing change, ask subgroups to list the changes they are experiencing in their organizations and their industries.

Assigning Roles

Roles can also be assigned in creative ways, rather than leaving the decision to the groups themselves. Suggest that the spokesperson, scribe, or discussion leader be the person whose birthday is closest to the day's date or who lives the closest to the training location.

Bob Pike of Creative Training Techniques in Minneapolis uses a fun finger-pointing technique. He asks people in their small groups to point their index fingers in the air; when he gives the signal, they are to point to someone in the group. The person who has the most fingers pointing at him or her is the spokesperson. To add a little more fun, variety, and surprise, the trainer can then tell the person who was just chosen to choose someone else. Come up with your own creative ideas. Let your imagination run wild!

Regaining Control

Sometimes trainers are afraid to have participants interacting with one another or moving into small groups because they are afraid of losing control and not being able to get the group's attention again. This is no problem with a little planning and communicating up front. First, be very clear and specific when telling participants what you want them to do; second, give them a time frame; and, finally, tell them what signal you are going to use to let them know when the time is up. There are many ways of regaining the audience's attention—both auditory and visual.

Auditory Signals Try Bob Pike's multiple clapping method. When he wants to call the group back to order, he asks them to clap once if they can hear his voice, and then he claps once. Next he asks them to clap twice if they can hear his voice, and he claps twice. Finally, he asks them to clap three times if they can hear him, and he claps three times. By that time, people have quieted down and refocused their attention on the trainer.

Use a variety of sounds, a train whistle, cow bell, siren, police whistle, sleigh bells, horn, or kazoo to regain the group's attention. When participants do not know what sound to expect they love the surprise.

Visual Signals Some trainers use visual signals such as turning the lights on and off or holding up a sign or object. Use any other idea you choose.

PROPS AND THEATRICAL TECHNIQUES

The use of props is becoming increasingly popular. Although props are visual aids and are used for a purpose similar to those discussed in Module Nine, they are included in this module because of their unique relationship to the theater and show business. Props can include hats, objects, or magic tricks—any object that enhances the message.

Using props is an easy and economical technique that will capture the audience's attention and help you communicate your message. Props appeal especially to the visual modality. They help reinforce a message by relating the visual image to the spoken word. The image will last long after the words are forgotten.

EXAMPLE OF USING PROPS

When I do a session on professional image, I begin by holding up two boxes of the same shape and size. One box is professionally wrapped with attractive paper and coordinating ribbon and bow; the other is wrapped in haphazard fashion in aluminum foil and tied with white curling ribbon. I ask the audience to indicate with a show of hands which package they would like to receive. Almost everyone chooses the attractive package. (Of course, there are always a few who choose the other.) I then ask one or two people to explain their preference for the professionally wrapped box to the others. They mention, of course, that it is more aesthetically appealing. This provides the segue into my points about professional image:

- Image is a matter of perception.
- Successful people first decide how they want to be perceived.
- Then they determine what to do to create that perception.

Props and Pointers

Coming up with ideas for props is not difficult. The key is to sit down and think about the learning points and brainstorm what objects might relate to or represent a particular message.

SAMPLE PROPS

For my session on coaching to improve workplace performance, I use a teddy bear dressed as an athletic coach in baseball cap and polo shirt with a whistle around his neck. I use my "coach" bear to introduce the concept that coaches in the work environment are similar to coaches in sports.

During management-development programs, I speak about employee motivation. To make my point about the different approaches to motivating employees, I bring in three props: a whip, a carrot dangling at the end of a stick, and a flowering plant. I show the whip to illustrate threats managers often make; the carrot represents incentive programs or promises of rewards as a motivational tool; the flowering plant is a metaphor for an environment in which people are motivated. A plant needs the right amount of water, light, heat, and fertilizer, and each plant requires different care. The same is true for people. Successful managers understand the different "care" required by each employee and create an appropriate environment accordingly. My "motivation" props are always a big hit. The participants frequently refer to the props throughout the session.

I also use a Slinky® magic spring to illustrate the importance of remaining flexible and adapting to change and a kaleidoscope to represent the changing environment. I use puzzle pieces for team building, giving each team member a puzzle piece that they hold until the end of the session, when I ask all of the team members to put their pieces together to complete the puzzle. I remind them that they are individuals, but that they must all come together to form the whole.

I often use a magic wand, "magic dust" (glitter), or a crystal ball. In a management-development session, I might mention that people are promoted to management positions and someone sprinkles "magic dust" or waves a magic wand and "abracadabra!," they now know how to manage.

A crystal ball can be used in a career-development program to make the point that many people expect to look into a crystal ball and see their future rather than taking control of their careers by developing plans and managing those plans.

Posters

Display posters of quotations related to the topic around the room to create a mood and generate interest in the topic. Quotations work well at the beginning of a session. Ask participants to choose one of the quotations and explain how it relates to them. The following quotes are appropriate for a time-management session:

- "Money lost can be replaced, but time lost is gone forever."
- "People who have half an hour to spend usually spend it with someone who hasn't."
- "Everybody has the problem of time; of all resources, it is the scarcest, the most perishable, and the most elusive."

Giveaways

A prop becomes even more effective and memorable if you use "giveaways" that coordinate with your theme. For example, you might give participants whistles in a coaching session; miniature Slinky®s to remind people to be flexible, or kaleidoscopes to help them look at things differently.

Use cube puzzles to represent problem solving. Give out small compasses in a session on goal setting to emphasize the importance of staying on course.

Give away buttons and stickers with words or slogans as a reminder of your theme or key learning points.

EXAMPLES OF RECOGNITION AND REWARDS

For a session for managers on motivating employees, I had buttons made that read, "I'm the greatest. My boss told me so!" as an example of an inexpensive way to recognize and reward employees. The managers were so excited about the button idea that they not only ordered those particular buttons to give to their employees, but came up with other button ideas and used them periodically to let employees know how important they were to the success of the organization.

Using Themes

Another way to add creativity to a workshop is to use a theme as a metaphor for the topic. Decorate the room and choose props and giveaways to support the theme. For example, the metaphor of a sailboat cruise can be used to represent team building, with the meeting room decorated in a nautical theme. When participants arrive, place leis around their necks and give out compasses to help them "stay on course." Give each person an eraser shaped like a sea creature and a roll of Lifesavers®.

Use an outer-space theme and have the room darkened and decorated with glow-in-the-dark stars and other celestial objects. If your session is about group problem solving or decision making, you might choose the NASA simulation from Teleometrics.

Using Imagination

Do not be afraid to take risks. Do something different. Use music. Have it playing as people come in the room and during breaks. Use balloons to show how managers can "celebrate" their employees' achievements. One word of caution: do not get carried away. Your creativity must not get in the way of your main purpose: a meaningful learning experience. Whatever you do should be an enhancement, not a distraction.

GAMES

Some training experts lump simulations and games into one category. Each will be addressed separately here, as they are two different (although related) techniques. The word "game" carries with it a different connotation, quite often an unfavorable one. A number of decision makers in organizations do not want their employees attending training sessions just to "play games." Unfortunately, in many instances, games have developed a bad reputation because they have not been used properly. Games, like other activities, must have an instructional purpose. They are tools for learning.

It is important for the trainer to evaluate a game well and link it to the "real world" through skillful conduct of the game and the facilitation process that follows the actual play. Game master Steve Sugar, principal of the Game Group in Ellicott City, Maryland, refers to instructional games as HOT (High-Outcome Techniques) training. He believes success depends on the facilitator's ability to know what to do, how to do it, and when to do it.

Instructional Games

To put it simply, an instructional game is an activity that involves rules and a repeating pattern of play. Reflecting a balance between knowledge and chance, an effective instructional game contains the following four C's:

- *Challenge.* By its very nature, a game is competitive and therefore has challenge, either built-in or assumed.
- *Chance.* Unlike a simulation or other experiential activities, a game includes an element of chance created by the roll of the dice or the luck of the draw.
- *Complication.* Complication is a factor involving both rules of play and questions that "test" the players' knowledge or skills.
- *Closure.* A game has a clear ending, determined by time or points, resulting in winners and losers.

A popular and versatile type of instructional game is known as a "frame game." A frame game involves selecting a well-known game structure and placing instructional material within that structure. Think of a frame game as a template, designed generically so that you can "load" or plug your own content into the game. There are two types of frame games: board games (Monopoly®, Trivial Pursuit®, Jeopardy®, Bingo®) and manual or pencil-and-paper games (Tic-Tac-Toe®, Scavenger Hunt®). You do not have to limit your use to popular and well-known games. There are a number of sources available for frame games that are easy to use. Game guru Sivasailam "Thiagi" Thiagarajan has a number of frame games as well as simulation games available on the market, as noted in Appendix B.

Advantages of Games

Like other experiential activities, instructional games can serve a number of purposes. Games serve two main purposes simultaneously: instruction and group development.

Instruction As an instructional technique, games can be used

- To assess the participants' knowledge or skill prior to the training.
- To teach new content: new information, concepts, and skills.
- To review or reinforce learning points for a particular segment or as a summary and review of the entire program.
- To assess how much the participants have learned.

Group Development Although the instructional purpose of the game should be of primary concern, at the same time, games can be used

- To break the ice and help people become acquainted with one another.
- To build rapport and create a comfortable learning climate.
- To build group cohesiveness by having people work in teams, resulting in collaboration as well as competition.
- To motivate participants and generate interest and enthusiasm for the topic.

Using Games

Results of a study conducted by James Kirk (1995) indicate that certain groups like games more than others. Kirk found that people under forty are more likely to enjoy the instructional use of games. Furthermore, supervisors or managers, those in sales and marketing positions, and professionals tend to respond favorably to games. Technicians, support staff, and operations workers are less likely to enjoy games.

Factors to Consider

The following factors must be taken into consideration when deciding whether or not to use an instructional game:

- *Time.* Steve Sugar estimates that it takes between seven and twelve minutes in development for every minute of playing time to create a game.
- *Cost.* Cost depends on a number of variables, including the complexity of the game, the number of game sets needed, production costs, purchasing costs, and, of course, how much time it takes to prepare.
- *Audience.* Consider the makeup of the group. Some games are more complex than others and will require some higher order thinking and application.
- *Enjoyment.* Although a game is a vehicle for learning, it should also be fun.

- *Adaptability*. The best instructional games are those that can be adapted easily to audience, subject, and time constraints.
- *User Friendly*. An instructional game must be easy to use and understand for both the participants and the facilitator.
- *Safety*. The game must be nonthreatening. Participants need to feel that it is okay to make a mistake.
- *Learning Objectives*. The instructional purpose must be clearly understood. Like all other activities, a game must lead to a learning outcome.

Adapting Games to Training Programs

After deciding to incorporate a game into the training design, you must actually build the game. The "master of instructional games," Steve Sugar, suggests the following approach:

Determine Your Objectives Decide why you are using a game. Are you using it to involve the participants? Add variety to the design? Energize the group? Make the learning interactive?

Select and Adapt a Frame Choose a frame that is user-friendly, adaptable, flexible, and challenging. Particularly if this is your first experience with a game, choose a frame that is familiar to both you and the participants, such as Jeopardy®, Bingo®, or Trivial Pursuit®. Participants from cultures outside the United States may not be familiar with these games, so be sure to learn about your audience before you choose a particular frame.

Develop the Rules Be clear about what people can and cannot do, how you will keep track of who is winning and losing, and when the game will be over. Write the rules so that they are easy to understand and are nonthreatening.

Load the Frame At this point, develop the questions specific to your content. This is time-consuming, so plan and manage your time accordingly.

Produce or Construct the Game This step involves creating the physical pieces of the game, including game board, sets of cards, game pieces, dice, etc. You can save some time by purchasing frame games that have been created for instructional purposes. (See Appendix B for some sources of games.)

For example, Steve Sugar has developed a great frame game called QUIZO! available from HRD Press. Using a bingo-type frame, the game comes with a pad of gamesheets, sheets for participants to use in recording their answers, game cards that the trainer uses to tell participants which space to mark off, and a facilitator's guide. The trainer decides on the content questions and, in this case, controls the game flow. Although this game is instructor-centered, it's a great way to review. I have used it for many different topics, including writing and grammar, train-the-trainer, and even leadership to review and reinforce cognitive learning.

A variation of this game that is participant-centered is Learnit! (also available from HRD Press). This game allows the participants to control the game flow. The game comes with a game board, game pieces, and generic cards that can be used for a number of topics such as stress management, customer service, and time management. You can, however, add your own cards to these or create all new cards for whatever your topic is.

Pilot the Game   Sometimes a game that looks good on paper fails miserably in the actual execution. Before going to great expense to produce slick materials, test it out on a small group of people representative of those who will actually play the game. As you observe and later debrief the game, ask yourself (and others) the following questions:

- "Were the participants involved?" "Was there a high level of participation among all the players?"
- "Were they learning?" "How do you know they were learning?"
- "Did they have fun?" "Were they animated and smiling?" "Were they energized?"
- "Were the questions and situations realistic?" "Whether the content was cognitive, behavioral, or affective, did it reflect what participants needed to know or do on the job?"
- "Was the environment nonthreatening?" "Was there an atmosphere of trust?" "Could people make mistakes without feeling embarrassed?"

Revise the Game   Based on the feedback you received from the pilot, you will probably need to make some revisions. Let the games begin!

Writing Game Questions and Items

When writing game questions, keep in mind that you want variety. Consider the following types of questions and items:

- *Short Answer.* These include many types: direct question (elicits a simple factual response), partial listing (elicits a list of characteristics), multiple choice, identification, definitions, and fill-in-the-blank.

- *Case Study*. These questions present hypothetical situations requiring the participant to explain briefly what he or she would do.
- *Role Play*. A role play requires the participant to actually do something that relates to the topic. For example, in a session on interpersonal skills, a role-play question might direct a participant to give feedback to one of his or her colleagues.
- *Discussion*. A discussion question requires the group to discuss something among themselves. In a session on business etiquette, the participants might discuss a female taking a male client to lunch and how to handle the check.
- *Activity or Process*. Questions are written on cards, reflect the element of chance, and include some non-content activities such as "lose a turn," "jump two spaces," or "go back a space."

Question cards should have questions on one side and answers as well as the rationale and references for the answers on the reverse. To maintain a balance between knowledge and chance, be sure to alternate between content and activity cards. Out of every five cards, one should be challenging; three, moderately challenging; and one, a "given."

Facilitating a Game

The biggest contributing factor to a game's failure is what the trainer does (or does not do) after the game is played. In a survey conducted by James Kirk (1995), 80 percent of training providers responded that they have received no structured training in game facilitation.

Games require the same care in processing as do other activities. If you follow the *"what?" "so what?" "now what?"* formula, along with the other processing tips introduced in Module Eight, your game will be successful. Be prepared, however, for mixed reactions. Because of the differences in learning styles, it is understandable and predictable that people will react differently. Some people may hate the game, while others think it is one of the best learning experiences they ever had.

So, do not become concerned unless you hear a lot of negative reactions.

Caveats

Trainers who have had little or no experience using an instructional game in training sessions are often very uncomfortable the first time. They are unnerved by the perceived loss of control, particularly if they have been delivering trainer-centered training. If the participants are really involved in the game, then the trainer is not even needed, except to answer the few questions that may arise, to observe the process, and to monitor the flow of the activity.

CREATIVE CLOSINGS

The way in which you bring a session or program to a close is very important. Think of it as a package tied with a neat little bow. Make sure to allocate adequate time to process the entire session or program. In a full-day session, allot thirty to forty minutes for closing activities.

Summarizing Techniques

Throughout the session, participants have been bombarded with information and activities. Before you send them on their way, help them pull it all together so that they leave the session with a clear understanding of the key learning points. Rather than taking on the responsibility of summarizing the session yourself, put the onus on the participants to think about what they have learned, synthesizing the content and experiences into key learning points. Remember that they will learn (and remember) better by doing rather than by being told.

Small-Group Summaries Divide the participants into subgroups. Give each subgroup a flip-chart sheet and markers and ask them to come up with a list of the key learning points from the session. Make it as specific as you want. For example, for a customer-service program, ask the small groups to pretend that they are going to be responsible for training new employees on the "dos" and "don'ts" of serving the customer. Ask them to develop a list of guidelines they would give new employees as a job aid and reminder of how to deliver quality service. After each group has developed its list, compare the lists, noting the similarities. They now have a summary checklist to take with them.

Full Circle A technique mentioned in Module Seven, "What Do You Want To Know?," uses Post-it™ Notes to keep track of questions participants have about the subtopics that will be addressed in the session. They place their questions on flip-chart sheets on the walls around the room. Ask participants to retrieve questions that were answered or addressed during the training program. Ideally, the wall will be empty.

However, a few may remain, generally questions that have absolutely nothing to do with the topic of the session. Occasionally, questions may remain that were touched on, but the participant who wrote the question does not recall the discussion. Either ask if anyone in the group remembers that question being addressed in some fashion or point it out for the participant yourself.

Self-Assessment

Also give participants an opportunity to reflect on how much they have personally grown or learned during the session. A great technique is to create a human continuum. This activity is adapted from a design called "Physical Self-Assessment" in *101 Ways To Make Training Active* (Silberman & Lawson, 1995).

For this activity, create two signs that represent the two extreme ends of a continuum and post them at opposite ends of a wall. For example, use "competent" and "clueless." Then ask participants to think about where they were at the beginning of the session or program relative to their knowledge, understanding, or skill level as it relates to the topic. Ask them to imagine the wall as a continuum and to stand up and place themselves where they think they were.

After the participants are in position, ask two or three to explain why they placed themselves where they did. Next ask them to think about where they see themselves now, at the end of the program, and to place themselves accordingly. Once again, ask a few to explain their positions. In most cases, you will find participants moving in varying degrees from "clueless" to "competent." This activity is a graphic way for both you and the participants to see how they have benefited from the training session.

Making Commitments

Mel Silberman tells trainers, "It's not what you give them, but what they take away that counts." Unless participants take what they learned and apply it to their own situations, the training will not be effective. To help ensure that training is transferred to the work environment, ask participants to develop their own action plans. Ask them to write down two or three action items they have as a result of the training. Ask them to write down not only what they are going to do, but how and when. Also ask them to consider what barriers they might anticipate and how they can overcome them. Exhibit 11.1 is an example of an action planning form used at the end of a management-development program.

EXHIBIT 11.1. Action
Plan

PERSONAL ACTION PLAN

1. What new thoughts, ideas, or insights have I gained from this program?

2. As a result of these new ideas, what specific thing(s) do I want to do differently on the job?

3. What things within my control could keep me from doing these things?

4. What outside barriers or obstacles could keep me from doing these things?

5. What can I do to overcome these internal and external barriers?

6. What help do I need from others in order to overcome these obstacles?

7. How will I know that I have succeeded (What results do I anticipate from my new behavior)?

Reflections

At the end of many training sessions, you can use a simple activity that combines self-assessment, action planning, and personal reactions. Put the following statements on a transparency or flip chart:

- The most important thing I learned in this session is. . . .
- As a result of this training, one thing I am going to do is. . . .
- What I liked best about this training session was. . . .

Then ask a few volunteers to share their responses to the items. It is a good way to obtain feedback and to help participants focus on or clarify in their own minds what was the most meaningful learning for them. Aside from being great feedback for the trainer, this technique helps participants leave with a sense of enjoyment and satisfaction with the learning experience.

✦ ✦ ✦

Module Twelve

Evaluating Training

LEARNING OUTCOMES

In this module, you will learn

- To use the four levels of evaluation
- To create evaluation tools
- To use the evaluation process to improve training effectiveness

---

WHY EVALUATE?

How many times have you heard someone say, "It was a great training program but . . . "? Unfortunately, that statement (or a variation) is spoken far too often and reflects a growing concern by both line managers and senior management that training is not always worth the investment of time and money. This attitude is also reflected in the actions of senior managers who cut training budgets first when times are tough.

Purposes of Evaluation

Following are some of the main reasons to evaluate:

- To determine whether the training achieved its objectives
- To assess the value of training programs
- To identify areas of the program that need improvement
- To identify the appropriate audience for future programs
- To review and reinforce key program points for participants
- To sell the program to management and participants

Linking Evaluation to the Needs Assessment

Clearly, needs assessment is critical to the success of any training initiative. It provides the basis for program development and establishes the criteria for measuring the success of the program after its completion. For evaluation to have any meaning, it must be tied to the needs-assessment process.

WHEN TO EVALUATE

Evaluation is an ongoing process, not just something that happens at the end of a session or program. Consider evaluation during the session, at the end, and after the participants return to the job.

During the Session

As people participate in skill practices, case studies, exercises, simulations, and other activities, observe the degree to which they have mastered the content.

At the End of the Session

Participants' evaluation questionnaires will indicate their personal reactions to the training session.

After the Training

A few weeks to several months after the session, observe the participants' job performance to determine whether they are applying what they learned to their work situations.

WHOM TO INVOLVE

Any category or number of people can be involved in the evaluation process, depending on what you want to know and what level of evaluation you conduct. The participants are directly involved because they are the customers whose level of satisfaction is being determined. The participants are the major source of information on how much they have actually learned in the training. In addition to the participants, involve others in the evaluation process. Survey or interview the participants' managers, their co-workers, peers, subordinates, or even customers or vendors. At some point, you may want to involve senior management.

HOW TO EVALUATE

The methods used for evaluation are pretty much the same as those used to gather data during the needs assessment. Trainers often ask, "Which method(s) should I use?" Unfortunately, there is no clear-cut answer. As Jane Holcomb

(1994) says in her book, *Make Training Worth Every Penny,* "use any method that works for you—any method at all that gives you the information you need."

WHAT TO EVALUATE

Before developing an evaluation process, be clear about what you want to evaluate. This is not as easy as it might seem. Do you want to evaluate how much the participants have learned? Or do you want to know what the participants thought about the program and you? Do you want to find out if the participants are applying what they learned on the job? If they are using the learned skills and information on the job, is their enhanced performance making a difference to the organization?

FOUR-LEVEL MODEL FOR EVALUATION

The most widely known model for evaluating training programs was introduced by Donald Kirkpatrick in 1959. It is regarded as a classic by training practitioners. Although all four levels of the model (*reaction, learning, behavior, results*) are important, you may not choose to evaluate at all four levels. Studies show that a vast majority of organizations evaluate reaction. A significantly high percentage measure learning as well. The evaluation or measurement of behavior lags behind the first two levels; evaluation of results finishes last.

Because behavior and learning are the most widely and commonly used levels of evaluation, this module focuses more heavily on conducting a Level 1 and a Level 2 evaluation. Recognize, however, that organizations are becoming increasingly more cost conscious, and the need to measure the effectiveness of training will continue to grow. With that in mind, Level 3 and Level 4 evaluation will be introduced, providing a basic overview of the concepts and principles. Should you need to undertake a comprehensive approach to evaluation, you will be able to make appropriate recommendations or respond confidently when someone asks you to prove that training gets results.

Figure 12.1 provides an overview of the four levels of evaluation.

Level 1: Reaction

Level 1 deals with participant reaction, that is, "customer" satisfaction. Level 1 evaluations are often referred to as "smile sheets," implying that participants' reactions are based on how much "fun" they had during the training session. For that reason, trainers frequently dismiss Level 1 evaluations as a waste of time.

On the contrary, Level 1 is an important first step in determining the success of a training program. Participants' reactions can help you determine

FIGURE 12.1. Measuring Training Results

	What	Who	When	How	Why
Level 1	*Reaction:* Did they like it?	Participants	End of program	"Smile Sheet"	Determine level of customer satisfaction; may indicate need for revision.
Level 2	*Learning:* What knowledge or skills did they retain?	Participants; Trainer	During, before/after program	Pretest/Post-Test; skills application through role plays, case studies, exercises	Identify if trainer has been successful in delivery of course content and achieving program objectives.
Level 3	*Behavior:* How are they performing differently?	Participants; Bosses; Subordinates; Peers	Three to six months after program completion	Surveys; Interviews; Observation; Performance Appraisal	Determine extent to which they have transferred what they learned in the classroom to the actual work situation.
Level 4	*Results:* What is the impact on the bottom line?	Participants; Control Group	After completion of Level 3 follow-up	Cost/Benefit Analysis; Tracking; Operational Data	Determine if benefits outweigh costs; ascertain degree of contribution of program to organizational goals.

the effectiveness of a program and how it can be improved. Kirkpatrick believes that you cannot bypass the first level because, as he puts it, "If they [participants] do not react favorably, they will not be motivated to learn" (Kirkpatrick, 1994).

What Level 1 Cannot Measure One of the problems with and the main cause of criticism of Level 1 evaluation is that it is too subjective and often becomes nothing more than a popularity contest. Before constructing a participant end-of-session evaluation form, understand what it cannot and is not intended to do: (1) It does not measure learning or the ability to apply learning on the job; (2) It also cannot measure changes in attitudes or beliefs; (3) Because it deals only with participants' perceptions and reactions, a Level 1 instrument can in no way measure organizational impact from the training; (4) Also, although frequently asked, participants cannot measure the trainer's knowledge. Think about it. How could the participants have any way of knowing what you do and do not know about the subject? Your ability to *communicate* or *demonstrate* your knowledge is an entirely different story.

Deciding What to Measure Before you design a Level 1 evaluation instrument, be clear about what you want to know, why you want to know it, and what you will do with the information. Do not ask for information about something you cannot change or have no intention of analyzing or reporting.

Designing an End-of-Session Evaluation Form

Categories. First decide what you want to measure and create questions or response items that address or fall into those categories, including many, if not all, of the following:

- Content
- Materials
- Instructional Methods
- Trainer
- Environment
- Logistics

It is also a good idea to provide an opportunity for respondents to make recommendations about how the program can be improved and also to express their overall reactions to the session.

Format. To counteract people's tendency to respond the same way to every item on a questionnaire or survey, use a variety of response formats. Choose at least four from the following options:

- *Two-choice questions with room for explanation or comments.* These would include responses such as "yes" or "no" and "agree" or "disagree," for example: "Did the course meet the stated objectives?   Yes   No"
- *Short answers.* These are written as open-ended questions and require the respondent to write a brief response instead of just checking a box, for example: "What parts of the workshop were most valuable/beneficial to you? Why?"
- *Complete the sentence.* With this item, the respondent is asked to complete a sentence, for example: "What I want/need to know more about is. . . ."
- *Ratings.* Participants respond to a question or statement using some type of scale or rating such as a Likert scale. The Likert scale measures both the direction (positive to negative) and intensity (strongly positive to strongly negative) of an individual's opinion or attitude, for example: "Today's session was an enjoyable and satisfying learning experience for me.

1	2	3	4	5	6	7	8
Strongly Disagree		Disagree		Agree		Strongly Agree"	

- *Rankings.* This type of item asks respondents to indicate priorities or preferences, for example: "Please rank each topic in order of its importance or relevance to your job from: 1 = most important to 5 = least important."
- *Checklist.* A checklist provides a "laundry list" from which participants can choose words that express their reactions, for example: "Check the phrases that describe your reaction to today's session:

    _____ Exceeded my expectations
    _____ Met my expectations
    _____ Fell short of my expectations"

A question could also be added focusing on the impact of the session on the participant, designed to obtain a deeper and more personal response, for example: "Imagine that a co-worker (or friend) of yours is thinking about attending this program. He or she asks you: 'What was the program like for you?' How would you respond?"

Evaluation Form Guidelines   Evaluation forms are more difficult to construct than you might imagine. Use the following guidelines:

- *Keep the form brief.* Participants should be able to complete it quickly.
- *Create a balance among the various types of information being collected.*

For example, do not ask five questions about the instructor and only two about content.

- *Obtain participants' immediate reactions.* Have participants complete the evaluation before they leave the room. This will ensure that you receive 100 percent of their feedback. It will also prevent "mob mentality" response, the possibility of several people getting together to discuss the group either before or while they are completing the evaluation.

Interviews In addition to end-of-session questionnaires, use interviews to increase the reliability of the data collected from the questionnaires. This method of data collection is quite flexible, allowing the interviewer to probe for more specific answers and to clarify questions or answers as needed. The method also allows the interviewer to record spontaneous answers and, therefore, obtain a more complete picture of the participants' reactions. The interviewer can explore in more detail the reactions gleaned from the questionnaires.

Plan to spend about thirty minutes per interview. You will not be able to interview every participant, so select a random sample. It is important to hold the interviews within one week of the session so that the experience is fresh in their minds. Through one-on-one interviews, you can further explore the reasons for participants' reactions and solicit suggestions for improvement. Either tape the interviews and have them transcribed, allowing you to analyze or interpret the responses more thoroughly, or simply take notes during the interviews.

When developing the interview questions, do not duplicate the questions on the written form. Instead, ask specific questions about the methods used or the content covered. For example, below are several questions about the methods used in a training session on leadership:

- "What feelings did you have about the methods used in the program?"
- "What did you like about the jigsaw design?"
- "What did you like about the learning tournament?"
- "What didn't you like about the jigsaw design?"
- "What didn't you like about the learning tournament?"

Level 2: Learning

Level 2 evaluation deals with what the participants actually learned during the training session. Kirkpatrick defines learning as the "extent to which participants change attitudes, improve knowledge and/or increase skill as a result of attending the program" (Kirkpatrick, 1994). It is far easier to determine what new knowledge or skills the participants acquired than the ways in which the training changed their opinions, values, and beliefs.

The three most appropriate methods used to evaluate learning are tests, observation, and interviews, with tests being the most frequent. See Figure 12.2 for a summary of the advantages and disadvantages of each method.

Tests Testing should be kept fairly simple. Many trainers give both a pretest and a post-test for an even more accurate picture of what the participants have learned. Developing tests or quiz questions is not easy.

Types of Tests. First, determine whether you want to construct subjective (short answer or essay) or objective (multiple choice or true/false) items or a combination of the two types. When constructing test items, consider the time needed to grade the test as well as the validity and reliability of each item. Make sure the test assesses the learning as specified in the learning objectives. When an item measures what it is supposed to measure, it has validity. Each test item must also be reliable, that is, give consistent results from one application to another.

FIGURE 12.2. Level 2 Evaluation Methods

Method	Advantages	Disadvantages
Objective tests (multiple-choice, matching, true/false, fill-in)	• Easy to score • Inexpensive to use	• Difficult to write • Time-consuming to write
Subjective tests (essay, short answer)	• Easy to write • Inexpensive to write	• Grading is time-consuming • Expensive to grade
Observation (observe behavior in class; demonstrate skills in practice sessions and learning activity)	• Immediate application • Lends itself to on-the-spot coaching and feedback	• Subjective, open to interpretation • Unable to spend adequate time observing behavior of all participants
Interviews (individual interviews shortly after the training; random sampling of participants	• Can gather more detailed information • Instant feedback	• Time-consuming; expensive • Must be tightly structured

Make sure the test is meaningful. Instead of asking for simple information or factual recall, ask questions that require the participants to apply or interpret what they learned in the session.

Test-Writing Guidelines. In most cases, you will probably choose to develop multiple-choice questions. They are easy to grade, but not necessarily easy to write. To help you construct a multiple-choice test that will provide valuable information about the participants' content mastery, consider the following guidelines:

- Avoid "all of the above" and "none of the above" options.
- Make sure the stem (the main part of the question) contains most of the information and defines the problem; place blanks for fill-ins near the end.
- Maintain grammatical consistency or parallel structure for both the stem and the answer choices.
- Try to create choices of equal length.
- Avoid ambiguity and reading difficulty by stating questions in the positive rather than in the negative.
- Keep the sentence stem simple and limit it to one idea.
- Use conversational language when phrasing the item and its choices.
- Arrange the questions in logical order.
- Do not give clues to the correct answer in the question.

Question Formats. All multiple-choice questions consist of a stem and a response. The stem presents a problem, asks a question, or takes the form of an incomplete statement. Responses include possible answers, all of which must be plausible. The greater the number of items, the better the test's reliability. Following are some formats to consider:

- *Correct Answer.* The correct-answer format asks a simple question to which there is only one correct answer. It is used primarily to test the recall of facts. This type of question is appropriate to test product knowledge, for example.
- *Best Answer.* With this type of question, there is more than one correct choice. Some or all of the choices may be correct to some degree. The best-answer question requires a higher level of thinking; the respondent must evaluate the choices and draw conclusions. This type of question can create many problems. Because the answer is open to interpretation, the test item can be challenged quite easily; you might find yourself arguing with the individual or group and most probably giving credit for other answers.

• *Combined Response*. This question is the most complicated and time-consuming for both the test writer and the test taker. The choices, one or more of which may be correct, are numbered. A second set of choices lists combinations of possible correct responses. This type of question assesses complex cognitive skills and the ability to analyze and evaluate. Exercise a great deal of thought when writing the item. Because of its complexity, the respondent will probably have to spend more time thinking about the item.

To gauge retention of the information learned in the program, administer another test several months following the training.

Observation Trainers can watch participants practicing and applying skills, tools, and techniques during the session. As the trainers observe participant behavior in skill practices, role plays, simulations, case studies, and other activities, they can get a good idea of what the trainees have really learned.

Interviews Shortly after the training, interview the participants and ask them what they learned in the session. Conduct the interviews within the week following the session.

Level 3: Behavior

The critical question answered by Level 3 evaluation is, "How has the training affected the way participants perform on the job?" Although both managers and training professionals agree that the success of a training program is determined by what the participants do with the information or skills back on the job, these results are often not obtained. Level 3 evaluation is both time-consuming and costly. It also requires good organizational and follow-up skills and processes.

Purpose of Level 3 Evaluation Use follow-up evaluation to do the following:

• Measure lasting results from the training
• Identify areas in which trainees show greatest and least improvement
• Compare follow-up and end-of-program responses

Follow-Up Guidelines   Use these guidelines for follow-up evaluation:

- *Prepare participants.* At the end of the training session, tell participants that you will be conducting a follow-up evaluation and what type of evaluation it will be.
- *If the training was not effective, find out why.* Encourage participants to identify reasons why they have not improved and what factors obstruct their progress. Sometimes there are factors that inhibit or prevent the application of the new knowledge and skills on the job. These barriers might include poor environmental conditions, lack of proper equipment, the supervisor, existing policies and procedures, or even the organizational climate.
- *Share follow-up evaluations with participants' managers or supervisors.* These individuals should know about program results and follow-up information and should be involved with the participants' practice and application of training.

Observations   The trainer or another designated observer can actually observe employees back on the job. Carefully watch employees as they perform routine job tasks and responsibilities. To facilitate the process and ensure consistency in the data gathering, create a checklist of desired behaviors and then observe whether or not the employee is demonstrating these behaviors.

For example, if you are observing someone who has recently attended a customer-service program, your list of customer-service behaviors might look like this:

_____   Smiles.

_____   Greets customer with "Good morning" or "Good afternoon."

_____   Uses the customer's name.

_____   Asks "How may I help you?"

_____   Offers additional assistance.

_____   Gives the customer choices.

_____   States what we can do, rather than what we cannot.

Interviews   Not only interview those who went through the training, but interview those who are affected by or closely associate with the program participants. Possible interviewees include the participants' managers, co-workers, customers, or subordinates. The interview questions must be carefully constructed and designed to focus on specific applications and behavioral changes.

Regardless of which evaluation method(s) you use, allow enough time for the behavioral change to take place. The length of time depends on the program, but three to six months should give the participants ample opportunity to apply what they learned and to develop new behaviors.

Surveys Surveys are a more efficient and less expensive way to find out if the participants are actually applying what they learned. Once again, do not limit your sources of information. Others who interact with those who participated in the training are often a more reliable source of feedback. Find out not only *if* trainees are using the training on the job but also *how* they are using it to perform better.

A control group is also helpful for a Level 3 evaluation. To validate your results, choose a control group of employees from the same function as the participants who received the training. Ask the members of the control group to complete the same surveys, questionnaires, and tests as those completed by the participants. Monitor their job performance and compare it with that of employees who received training.

Level 4: Results

Level 4 evaluation measures the impact of the training on the organization. Ideally, it shows how the training has contributed to accomplishing organizational goals and objectives—business results. If an organization chooses to conduct a Level 4 evaluation, the areas of measurement must be the same as those identified in the needs assessment.

To measure training's impact on the bottom line, return to the data gathered during the needs assessment. Determine the critical success factors up front. Results measured could include any of the following or any measurable item:

- Production output
- Sales
- Operating costs
- Customer satisfaction
- Quality standards
- Safety record
- Turnover rate
- Absenteeism
- Employee grievances
- Employee satisfaction
- Budget variances
- Promotions

Level 4 evaluation is both difficult and time-consuming. It can also be quite costly. It is difficult to measure because of the many variables that can come into play after the participants leave the session. For these reasons, a Level 4 evaluation is not appropriate for all training. From a practical standpoint, consider Level 4 for those programs that are near and dear to senior management and have been identified as a top priority.

Because of the complexity of Level 4 evaluation and how infrequently it is used, it is addressed here only in very basic terms—just enough to give an idea of what it involves and the purpose it serves. To explore Level 4 in more detail, refer to the listings in Appendix B, including Jack Phillips, Jane Holcomb, Donald Kirkpatrick, and Dana Gaines Robinson and James Robinson.

As a starting point, test your current knowledge of measurement terms by matching the terms in the left-hand column with the correct definitions in the right-hand column below (see Appendix A for the correct answers):

Term	*Definition*
_____ 1. ROI	a. Survey data of employee attitudes
_____ 2. Direct Costs	b. Salaries and benefits paid to participants for the time they are attending the program
_____ 3. Indirect Costs	c. Expenses for creating the training program
_____ 4. Overhead	d. Involves quantity, quality, cost, time; easily converted to monetary value
_____ 5. Development Costs	e. Costs of shared resources such as heating and building maintenance
_____ 6. Hard Data	f. Expenses of operating the training department that are not directly related to any training program
_____ 7. Soft Data	g. Mathematical formula for calculating the difference between cost and value
_____ 8. Compensation for Participants	h. Costs related to the delivery of the training program, such as materials and trainer's salary

ACCOUNTABILITY FOR TRAINING

Throughout the business world, accountability for all functions is increasing. Staff functions such as training are expected to prove their contributions and value to the organization. Top executives are demanding that training departments offer proof of their worth or take budget cuts. Two approaches to measuring the value of training are covered below: (1) cost/benefit analysis and (2) return on investment.

Cost/Benefit Analysis

Cost/benefit analysis looks at the total cost to produce a training program and attempts to quantify the benefits. Costs include everything from the needs assessment through design, development, delivery, and follow-up. Both direct and indirect costs are used to determine the total cost of the program. As Figure 12.3 shows, determining training costs is complex.

Total benefits of the program may be reduced costs or increased revenues directly attributable to the training. In many cases, however, benefits can only be estimated. Subtract the total costs from the total benefits to find the net benefit of the training program. A program is considered a financial success if the costs are lower than the benefits.

Return on Investment

The return on investment simply shows what the payback is for the training program. To determine return on investment, wait three to six months or longer for operational results. The formula for determining return on investment: ROI = net program benefits/program costs × 100. Stated simply, if training programs fail to show a reasonable return on the company's investment, future (or even current) training initiatives are at risk.

SIGNIFICANCE OF THE EVALUATION PROCESS

Evaluation is a complex issue. For one reason, many variables enter into the equation. No matter how hard you try to fine-tune the evaluation process, the reality is that effects can only be estimated, and economic benefits cannot be calculated precisely. As the role of training departments continues to change and trainers reposition themselves as performance consultants, there will be more pressure to measure the effectiveness of training. The good news, however, is that the field of training and development continues to grow at a rapid pace. This trend will continue to provide many opportunities for training professionals, both internal and external, to make an impact on the growth and development of individuals and organizations throughout the world.

✦ ✦ ✦

FIGURE 12.3. Determining Training Costs

DIRECT COSTS			
	People	*Facilities*	*Materials*
Design and Development	Salaries, benefits, travel for: Course development & clerical support or Consultant fee and expenses or Costs of certifying in-house trainer for purchased programs		Marketing brochures Participant materials Instructor manual Purchased resource materials Purchased program
Delivery	Salaries, benefits, travel for: Trainer(s) Participants (average salary) Clerical support Consultant fees and expenses	Room rental Equipment rental Refreshments	Notebooks Folders Tent cards Paper Pencils/pens Flip charts Handouts Film rental/purchase Transparencies/slides Stationery items Certificates Books Reprints
Evaluation	Salaries, benefits, travel for: Training personnel Participants Clerical support Bosses Subordinates Peers		Surveys Questionnaires
INDIRECT COSTS			
Training space Custodial services Utilities Postage	Telephone Computer time Equipment Equipment depreciation		Maintenance/repair Support services

Appendix A
Answers to Exercises

Exhibit 3.2: Learner-Centered or Information-Centered Behavior

1. IC
2. IC
3. LC
4. IC
5. IC
6. IC
7. IC
8. LC
9. IC
10. IC
11. IC
12. LC
13. LC
14. IC
15. LC
16. LC
17. LC
18. IC

MODULE EIGHT

Seating Arrangements

1. Classroom
2. Cluster
3. Horseshoe
4. Single Square or Round
5. Semi-Circle or Full Circle
6. Conference
7. Chevron

Active Knowledge Sharing

- 125 to 150 words per minute
- 400 to 500 words per minute
- 80 percent; 45 precent
- 83 percent sight
- 11 percent sound
- 6 percent all other senses combined

Pretest

1. F
2. F
3. T
4. F
5. T

MODULE TWELVE

Term Definitions

1. g
2. h
3. f
4. e
5. c
6. d
7. a
8. b

Appendix B

Recommended Resources

Books

Broad, M.L., & Newstrom, J.W. (1992). *Transfer of training*. Reading, MA: Addison-Wesley.

Cohen, G., Eyseneck, M.W., & Le Voi, M.E. (Eds.). (1986). *Memory: A cognitive approach*. Philadelphia, PA: Open University Press.

Eitington, J.E. (1984). *The winning trainer*. Houston, TX: Gulf.

Gilley, J.W., & Coffern, A.J. (1984). *Internal consulting for HRD professionals*. Burr Ridge, IL: Irwin Professional Publishing.

Kirkpatrick, D.L. (1994). *Evaluating training programs: The four levels*. San Francisco: Berrett-Koehler.

Mager, R.F., & Pipe, P. (1984). *Analyzing performance problems*. Belmont, CA: David S. Lake Publishers.

Mill, C.R. (1980). *Activities for trainers: 50 useful designs*. San Francisco: Jossey-Bass/Pfeiffer.

Newstrom, J.W., & Scannell, E.E. (1980). *Games trainers play*. New York: McGraw-Hill.

Pfeiffer, J.W. (Ed.) (1972–1998). The *Annual* series. San Francisco: Jossey-Bass/Pfeiffer.

Phillips, J. (1983). *Handbook of training evaluation and measurement methods*. Houston, TX: Gulf.

Reynolds, A. (1993). *The trainer's dictionary: Terms, acronyms, initials, and abbreviations*. Amherst, MA: HRD Press.

Robinson, D.G., & Robinson, J. (1989). *Training for impact.* San Francisco: Jossey-Bass.

Rossett, A. (1987). *Training needs asssesment.* Englewood Cliffs, NJ: Educational Technology Publications.

Scannell, E.E., & Newstrom, J.W. (1983). *More games trainers play.* New York: McGraw-Hill.

Scannell, E.E., & Newstrom, J.W. (1991). *Still more games trainers play.* New York: McGraw-Hill.

Silberman, M. (1980). *Active training: A handbook of techniques, designs, case examples, and tips.* San Francisco: Jossey-Bass/Pfeiffer.

Silberman, M. (1992). *Twenty active training programs: Vol. I.* San Francisco: Jossey-Bass/Pfeiffer.

Silberman, M. (1994). *Twenty active training programs: Vol. II.* San Francisco: Jossey-Bass/Pfeiffer.

Silberman, M., & Lawson, K. (1995). *101 ways to make training active.* San Francisco: Jossey-Bass/Pfeiffer.

Sparhawk, S. (1994). *Identifying targeted training needs.* Irvine, CA: Richard Chang & Associates.

Video Producers

American Media Incorporated
4900 University Avenue
West Des Moines, IA 50266–6769

CRM Films
2215 Faraday Avenue
Carlsbad, CA 92008

Video Arts
8614 West Catalpa Ave.
Chicago, IL 60656
800-553-0091

Assessment Instruments, Simulations, and Games

Human Synergistics
39819 Plymouth Road
Plymouth, MI 48170
313-459-1030

HRDQ (formerly Organization Design and Development)
2002 Renaissance Boulevard, Ste. 100
King of Prussia, PA 19406–2756
800-633-4533

HRD Press
22 Amherst Rd.
Amherst, MA 01002
800-822-2801

Xicom
Sterling Forest
Tuxedo, NY 10987
800-759-4266

Props, Toys, and Training Tools

Creative Learning Tools
P.O. Box 37
Wausau, WI 54402
715-842-2467

Creative Training Techniques Press
7620 West 78th Street
Minneapolis, MN 55439
800-383-9210

The Trainer's Warehouse
89-I Washington Avenue
Natick, MA 01760
800-299-3770

✦ ✦ ✦

Appendix C

Criteria for Selecting Packaged Programs

Use the following checklist to evaluate packaged programs. Choose the criteria that are important to you and your organization. Then apply each criterion to the program you are evaluating to make the best decision for the particular situation. This is also a valuable tool for justifying the cost of purchasing a program.

- Program is based on solid research.
- Absolute, bottom-line price is reasonably low.
- Cost/value ratio is low.
- Payment flexibility, discounts, etc., are available.
- Vendor has good reputation in the field.
- You *purchase to own* course materials, versus renting/leasing them.
- Vendor makes client referrals available for contact.
- You have good relationship with vendor's representative.
- Vendor's representative is knowledgeable.
- Program can be customized.
- Industry-specific version is available.
- Program is time-tested, has been around a while.
- Program is new or updated.
- You have previously worked with vendor.
- Quality of the vendor's formal proposal is high.
- Convenient access to vendor is possible.
- Quality of course materials is high.
- Leader's guide is easy to follow.
- Course materials are immediately available.

- Specific participant is targeted, i.e., new or experienced.
- Program has unique concept: It's different.
- Materials are easy to use with few problems likely starting up.
- Program's objectives match yours.
- Vendor provides start-up support.
- Flexibility allowed with participant group size.
- Line manager could present program.
- Program is entertaining/engaging.
- Program is content-rich.
- Overall quality of program is high.
- Vendor offers other programs/services.
- You can reprint.
- Program is likely to be critiqued highly.
- Variety of media are used.
- Reinforcement modules are available.

◆ ◆ ◆

References

Clark, R.C., & Taylor, D. (1994, July). The causes and cures of learner over-load. *Training & Development*, pp. 38–43.

Cripple, G. (1996). Instructional styles diagnosis inventory. In *The 1996 annual: Volume 1, training.* San Francisco: Jossey-Bass/Pfeiffer, pp. 147–160.

Hall, J. (1994). *NASA moon survival task.* The Woodlands, TX: Teleometrics International.

Holcomb, J. (1994). *Make training worth every penny: On-target evaluation.* San Francisco: Jossey-Bass/Pfeiffer.

Ingham, J., & Dunn, R. (1993). The Dunn and Dunn model of learning styles: Addressing learner diversity. In J.W. Pfeiffer (Ed.), *The 1993 annual: Developing human resources.* San Francisco: Jossey-Bass/Pfeiffer.

Jacobs, R.T., & Fuhrmann, B.S. (1984). Learning-style inventory. In J.W. Pfeiffer & L.D. Goodstein (Eds.), *The 1984 annual for group facilitators.* San Francisco: Jossey-Bass/Pfeiffer.

James, W.B., & Galbraith, M.W. (1995, January). Perceptual learning styles: Implications and techniques for the practitioner. *Lifelong Learning*, pp. 20–23.

Johnson, D.W., Johnson, R.T., & Smith, K.A. (1991). *Cooperative learning: Increasing college faculty instructional productivity.* ASHE-ERIC Higher Education Report No. 4. Washington, DC: The George Washington University, School of Education and Human Development.

Keller, J.M. (1983). Motivational design of instruction. In C.M. Reigeluth (Ed.), *Instructional-design theories and models: An overview of their current status.* Hillsdale, NJ: Erlbaum.

Kirk, J. (1995). *Trainers' use of games: Some preliminary explorations.* (Unpublished manuscript). Cullobee, NC: Author.

Kirkpatrick, D. (1994). *Evaluating training programs: The four levels.* San Francisco: Berrett-Koehler.

Knowles, M. (1990). *The adult learner: A neglected species.* (4th ed.). Houston, TX: Gulf.

Kolb, D. (1991). *Learning styles inventory.* Boston: McBer & Company.

Lawson, K. (1998). *Involving your audience: Make it active.* Needham Heights, MA: Allyn and Bacon.

Meyers, C., & Jones, T.B. (1993). *Promoting active learning: Strategies for the college classroom.* San Francisco: Jossey-Bass.

Murrell, K.L. (1987). The learning-model instrument. In J.W. Pfeiffer (Ed.), *The 1987 annual: Developing human resources.* San Francisco: Jossey-Bass/Pfeiffer.

Oppenheim, L. (1981). *Studies of the effects of the use of overhead transparencies on business meetings.* Philadelphia, PA: Wharton Applied Research Center, Wharton School, University of Pennsylvania.

Pescuric, A., & Byham, W.C. (1996, July). The new look of behavior modeling. *Training & Development,* pp. 24–30.

Phillips, K.R. (1987). *Coaching skills inventory.* King of Prussia, PA: Organization Design and Development.

Scannell, E.E., & Newstrom, J.W. (1983). *More games trainers play.* New York: McGraw-Hill.

Silberman, M. (1998). *Active training.* (2nd ed.). San Francisco: Jossey-Bass/Pfeiffer.

Silberman, M., & Lawson, K. (1995). *101 ways to make training active.* San Francisco: Jossey-Bass/Pfeiffer.

Sterns, H., & Doverspike, D. (1988). Training and developing the older worker: Implications for human resource management. In H. Dennis (Ed.), *Fourteen steps in managing an aging work force.* Lexington, MA: Lexington Books.

Thomas, K., and Kilmann, R. (1974). *The Thomas-Kilmann conflict mode instrument.* Sterling Forest, NY: Xicom.

Vogel, D.R., Dickson, G.W., Lehman, J., & Shuart, K. (1996). *Persuasion and the role of visual presentation support: The UM/3M study.* Minneapolis, MN: Management Information Systems Research Center, School of Management, University of Minnesota.

Walters, L. (1993). *Secrets of successful speakers.* New York: McGraw-Hill.

White, K. (1996, September). Ten most frequently asked questions and their answers. *Training & Development,* pp. 26–30.

Zemke, R., & Armstrong, J. (1997, May). How long does it take? *Training,* pp. 69–79.

◆ ◆ ◆

Index